Batik in Many Forms

Laura Adasko & Alice Huberman

Batik
In Many Forms

Photography by Frank Conaway

William Morrow and Company, Inc./New York

DESIGNED BY ANN MEZEY

1 2 3 4 5   79 78 77 76 75

Library of Congress Cataloging in Publication Data

Adasko, Laura.
   Batik in many forms.

   1. Batik.   I. Huberman, Alice, joint author.
II. Title.
TT852.5.A3   746.6   74-16376
ISBN 0-688-00340-0

TO MEL

Acknowledgments

We are constantly creating a design for our lives just as we are creating designs in batik. And the design is always changing, always growing. That is the external excitement and expansion of our lives' designs. What we do and who we do it with define the design, color it, and extend it into new patterns and undiscovered lands. That is how we continue to meet ourselves and to be continuously reborn.

This book has become a part of the design of our lives. It has been written through the time we've spent with many people; people who allowed us to be ourselves and who loved us. They were supportive, patient, and confident even when we hesitated and questioned. They were giving and there for us .even when we were too tired, too overwhelmed, too uncertain to be there for ourselves.

That is why, in many ways, this book belongs to all those people who were there: our families, our friends, our teachers. It is impossible to begin to thank them for something so precious.

Contents

List of
Color Illustrations

Introduction

This is a book about batik. We are writing it because batik is something we love to do, something that is part of our lives which we would like to share with others. We feel many people—perhaps you!—could find the same joy and excitement in pursuing this creative craft that we have found, and if through this book you were to discover batik, we would be very happy indeed. We hope that in writing *Batik in Many Forms* we are able to communicate the personal experience of self-discovery and self-expression which we have found in doing batik.

Batik does not require formal training. It does not require that you be an artist or designer, or even that you attend special classes in the process itself. Neither of us was specially educated in the batik medium; in fact, our formal training had gone in quite different directions until we began to experiment with batik on our own. What you do need for batik is an openness, a desire to work with your hands, a desire to create something, to express yourself, to explore something unknown. The techniques of the craft and the materials used can be learned about by reading books, but will really become known and developed by you only in the actual experience of doing batik.

WHAT IS BATIK?

People who do batik are often annoyed by such innocent remarks as "Oh, that's a nice tie-dye," or "I just love hand-printed fabrics!" Actually, batik is as unrelated to the processes of tie-dyeing and printing fabrics as it is to weaving and embroidery. It involves completely different materials, tools, and techniques, and the results are also entirely unique. Batik is a process of creating designs on fabric by applying hot, liquid wax to cloth and then dyeing it. The molten wax is applied to the cloth with brushes or a special batik instrument called a *tjanting*, and as it is applied the wax penetrates the cloth and hardens. The cloth is then submerged in dye. When the cloth is dyed, the wax acts as a *resist*, preventing the dye from entering the cloth in the waxed areas and thus creating a design on the fabric. The process of painting wax onto the cloth and dyeing it can be repeated many times, each time adding more of the design and a new color to the cloth. When the design is finished, the wax is removed. Batik requires fabrics of natural fibers such as cotton, linen, silk, and wool, wax (usually a combination of paraffin and beeswax), and cold-water dyes.

BATIK AND OTHER HAND-PRINTING METHODS

Batik is distinguished from all other methods of hand-designing fabrics first by the fact that it is the only process using wax to create the design on the cloth. *Tie-dye* does not use wax, but is a process of folding or twisting cloth and tying it at different points with rope, thread, cord, or rubber bands. The cloth is then dyed and the ties and folds form a resist to the dye, creating a design. In tie-dye the design can be changed and varied by the use of different tying materials, by the spacing of the ties, by altering the folds, and by the number of times the cloth is dyed.

Silk-screening does not involve the use of wax either. Silk-screening is a process of printing a design on fabric (or paper) by blocking out parts of a mesh screen with a stencil and, with a squeegee, forcing pigment, ink, or dye through the mesh screen onto the fabric. The ink or dye will go through only the open parts of the screen and appear on the fabric; the stencil will block the ink or dye. In silk-screening you do not make a design directly on fabric. Rather, you make a design on the screen, and the screen can be used over and over again to reproduce the design on many yards of fabric. This method is quite unlike that of batik, in which the design is made directly on the cloth itself.

Each time a batik is made, the design must be created anew, even if it has been used before. In batik, in fact, a design is never exactly the same no matter how many times it is used. Silk-screening also differs from batik in that it does not involve submerging cloth in dye. As a result the dyes often do not penetrate the cloth fully but tend to sit on the surface. In batik the immersion of the cloth in dye means that the dye will fully penetrate, no matter how thick the fabric.

Block printing, another method of hand-designing fabric, is quite dissimilar in process from batik. While in batik the design is made directly on the fabric by painting with molten wax to create a resist, in block printing the design is carved into a wooden or linoleum block, ink is rolled onto the block, and then the block is pressed repeatedly on the cloth. The block leaves an impression of the design on the fabric.

Hand painting of fabric also does not require the use

of wax to create a design. It is a process of applying dye directly to fabric with a brush, often using a resin to outline the design.

It is obvious from this short review of methods for hand-designing fabric that *wax* is the most distinctive attribute of the batik process. And it is the wax that creates the special mark of batik—the *crackle*. Batik is always easily identified by its tiny, fine, veinlike lines which appear throughout the design. These lines are formed by the cracking of the wax as the cloth dyes, thus allowing the dye to penetrate into the cracks. These cracks will always appear in a batik and are its distinguishing characteristic. So if you see crackle, you know it is a batik!

Batik also differs from other methods of hand-designing fabric in its use of cold-water dyes. No other method requires the use of cold-water dyes because none involves the use of wax. In batik the cloth has to be dyed at cool temperatures because if it were dyed at temperatures above 110 degrees, the wax would start to melt and the design would be lost. The use of cold-water dyes also means that only natural fibers can be used in batik, since synthetics cannot take color at low temperatures. In other dye processes, you are not limited to these fibers. Therefore as you can see, batik is distinguished from other hand-designing processes by its use of wax, natural fibers, and cold-water dyes.

THE HISTORY OF BATIK

Batik is an ancient craft. Although its exact date and place of origin are unknown, most sources say that batik

PLATE 1: *Detail of Batik. Design by Alice Huberman on silk broadcloth. Note the "crackle."*

16

was found in ancient Egypt as early as 1500 B.C., and early relics of batik have been found in Peru dating back to ancient times. It is also known to have existed in early China and Japan (eighth century) and in ancient India. Some say that it was first developed in India and spread west from there; others claim that it originated in China, moving to Malaysia and, through India, to the West. In any case, today batik can be found in India, China, Japan, Africa, and Indonesia, as well as in Europe and America.

Whatever its origin, batik was most highly developed by the Javanese of Indonesia, beginning in the thirteenth century, and it continues to flourish there today. The art of Indonesian batik was first explored by the ladies of the ruling class, who had time to spend six or eight weeks designing and waxing one sarong. Gradually, however, the popularity of this technique spread and workers or servants became involved, especially when the trade markets for batiks began to develop in the seventeenth century.

Traditionally, Javanese women designed and waxed the fabric, using the special tool called the *tjanting*, and men did the dyeing. The designs came from natural forms, but over the centuries became stylized symbols and motifs, each with its own name and meaning.

Dyes were also established by tradition and, until the late nineteenth century, were natural dyes. The first color used was indigo blue, followed by red and yellow; and these three colors, dyed in combination, became the traditional colors in Javanese batik for centuries. Usually, a Javanese batik is dyed twice, each color having its own meaning, often indicating its regional or family origin.

PLATE 2: *Traditional Caftan. Batik by Alice Huberman on silk chiffon. Loaned by Mrs. Melvin Siegel, Minneapolis.*

17

The traditional Javanese method, still to be found in use today, is applied to a cloth about six yards in length (the length of a sarong) and requires many steps.

"To begin with, the fabric is given a special pretreatment. It is first scoured and then kneaded with peanut oil or another vegetable oil to make it receptive to the resist paste, which should penetrate and adhere well. At the same time this treatment is also indispensable for the subsequent dyeing process since it ensures satisfactory penetration and absorption of the dyestuff by the fibre. . . . Following the kneading in oil the fabric used to be treated in a suspension of rice straw ash in water to remove excess oil. . . .

"The batik printer—generally a woman—sits cross-legged in front of the length of cloth, which hangs from the gawangan, a wooden or bamboo stand. With the 'tjanting' she applies the pattern to the fabric in molten wax. . . .

"Often the outlines of the pattern are roughly sketched first on the fabric before being drawn in wax. But the experienced and skillful amongst the batik printers know their patterns by heart and draw free-hand from memory. When one side is finished, the fabric is held up against the light and the pattern is drawn on the reverse. Now the fabric is ready for dyeing, the first color generally being indigo. The dye recipes are traditional family recipes often containing very peculiar ingredients indeed, for instance brown palm sugar, fermented cassava starch, various types of banana and even ground chicken meat.

"After dyeing, the wax must be removed from the fabric. A large portion of it comes off by mechanical treatment, but a more reliable method is that of treating the fabric in boiling water. This may be followed by as many applications of wax and dyeing operations as are necessitated by the design of the article." [From "Coloristic Aspects of African Prints" by Ing W. Kretzschmar]

The development of trade routes by the Portuguese and later the Dutch in the sixteenth and seventeenth centuries had significant consequences for the craft of batik in general, and for the indigenous craft in Indonesia in particular. As markets with Europe and Africa developed, real industry developed in Indonesia. With the introduction of a copper handstamp tool called a *tjap* in the nineteenth century, batik designs could be reproduced much more quickly. In the late nineteenth century chemical dyes were also introduced, so that by the twentieth century Indonesians were able to produce imitation batik fabrics in great quantities.

With the chartering of the Dutch East India Company in 1602, Indonesian batik traveled to Europe and from there to Africa. As batik spread through Europe in the seventeenth and eighteenth centuries, its popularity increased and a new craft as well as a new industry developed. At first, budding textile industries, particularly in England, tried to reproduce the batik look through an industrial printing process. This process never met with much success, because imitating crackle by mechanical means proved difficult and expensive. By the twentieth century, however, such imitations were "perfected," though they never really had the look and richness of true batik.

Simultaneously with the development of the batik industry, the true handcraft also flourished. Europeans began to explore this medium, giving to it their own individual expression and experimenting with the form. The Art Nouveau era that began in the 1890's produced beautiful and highly original batik fabrics, particularly in France, England, and Germany. These fabrics were highly popular and were used for everything from elaborate haute-couture evening dresses to window curtains.

Today batik is experiencing another renaissance. Artists are experimenting with ancient techniques for batik as well as adopting new, more painterly methods. As Dona Z. Meilach describes in her book *Batik and Tie-. Dye*, "The trend is to decorate the fabric any way the artist envisions; to apply design by any method, traditional or innovative, and even depart from standard procedures. Batik no longer is considered a 'pure' art, but one which can be combined with other media and methods. The driving force for the artist is to apply the technique for the end desired."

So whether today's batik fabrics are used in the traditional ways, for clothing, or in newer ways, for furniture upholstering, batik "paintings" or wall hangings, or even three-dimensional batik art forms, it is clear that the art of batik is still alive and, in fact, reborn—and waiting for even fresher developments.

BATIK AS AN EXPERIENCE

Batik is a creative process, involving the development and control of special techniques and materials—namely, dyes, wax, and fabric. In this book we hope to give you a basic knowledge of the batik process by describing, as completely as we know, all aspects of the materials used, technical considerations and limitations, the various steps or stages involved, and the design possibilities and problems inherent in batik.

But beyond these considerations, and even within these considerations, we hope we can communicate to you the experience itself, which is much more than just the skills or technique of doing batik. Batik is an individual, personal experience. It is a way of having contact with yourself, of learning new things about your own possibilities, of exploring and expanding your own limits. It is a medium that allows endless exploration of design, color, fabric, and function. Each time you do a batik, you can have a new experience—by changing the design, working with new colors or fabrics, or using the batik in another form. The experience of making a velveteen pillow or a lampshade, a silk blouse or a hanging for the wall—each will be totally unique in terms of design, skill, and limitations, even though the basic process is the same. The dynamics of working in this medium are radically changed by introducing a new fabric, a different design consideration, or another functional application. Because of this the experience of doing batik is never boring, never repetitive, never exactly the same, never exhausted of its potentiality. Quite simply, the experience is always exciting!

Batik is an immediate process, a fact which contributes to its excitement. At each step of the process something new emerges which you will see immediately. The design begins to take shape with the first waxing, becomes alive with the first dyeing, and each step thereafter adds a new dimension that you can see. You and your work constantly interact, changing in the process. And because you work quickly, getting direct feedback from your work, an element of spontaneity is always present in batik.

The dynamic and exhilarating quality of batik is increased by the ever-present element of noncontrol. No matter how much skill and control you may develop, the medium exerts a will of its own, and it is really the acceptance of its power separate from you which gives you and your work unrealized potential. Each time you dye your cloth, you will achieve results not always planned for or intended. The amount of crackle, the way in which the cracks are formed on a particular piece, can never be fully determined. And even though, with each step, you gain a sense of definition, you can never envision the totality of the piece until the wax is finally removed. The work always remains mysterious and unknown, as if a film or veil exists between you and the batik, a film created by the wax disguising the true colors underneath. When the wax is removed, the work is unveiled, and finally you see the work in its true form.

Whatever the final form, a batik always contains life. It is an expression of your life and it has a relationship to your life in the function it serves. Batik always establishes a connection to you through its use, whether it hangs on your wall and brings color to the room, or it hangs on you.

Batik is truly a craft of many forms. And as a result it is also a craft that can give to you infinite forms of experience through which you can discover and explore yourself.

PART I
THE BASIC MATERIALS OF BATIK

The Basic
Materials of Batik

In any craft there are always a few basic materials with which one constantly works: in ceramics, one works with clay and glaze; in weaving, looms and wool; in jewelry, metals and stones; in embroidery, fabric and thread and needles; and in batik, one works with fabric, wax, and dyes. These basic materials of batik define the possibilities and limitations of the craft. They are the raw materials which are processed and refined as one works.

In the beginning it is helpful to become familiar with the nature and characteristics of the materials with which you work. This familiarity allows you to make intelligent choices, to see the limitations inherent in the medium, and to understand how to develop skill and craft in your work. It is much like making a good apple pie. First you must know about apples—which ones are best for cooking in terms of flavor and texture. Then you must know about spices—how they affect the flavor of apples, which ones seem to complement their flavor. And finally, you must learn the proportions of flour, butter, and water to obtain the proper consistency of crust. Once you know about the ingredients, you can then put them together successfully and even experiment or change them to improve the result.

The more you know about the materials with which you work, the more you will be able to do and the more you will know what not to do. Through an understanding of fabric, wax, and dyes, you will be able to expand and explore the batik medium by new combinations of materials, by using different dyes, or new fabrics, or another mixture of wax. As you begin to understand the interrelationship and interaction of the materials in batik, you will begin to discover new possibilities and choices, avoid and eliminate the impossibilities, and thus direct your energies in a positive and satisfying way.

Fabric

Since batik is a method of hand-designing fabric, a major consideration in pursuing the craft is the fabric with which you will work. The fabric you select in large part determines the result you achieve. Selecting the *right fabric* for the *right design* and the *right function* is certainly of the utmost importance.

Certain fabrics with a particular weight, texture, and sheen may enhance one design but take away from another. The intensity of color achieved with certain fabrics may be suitable for one design but not for another. One fabric may be suitable for one purpose or function (e.g., a blouse) but not for another (e.g., a pillow). So the decision about fabric is a critical one and should be made with care and consideration.

In batik one can work with any natural fiber, i.e., wool, silk, cotton, or linen. In addition some batik craftsmen have been able to work successfully with a few synthetics such as rayon or acetate. However, synthetics present certain problems in waxing and dyeing, and they

27

do not have the richness or aliveness of natural fibers. We do not like synthetics and so we do not work with them and have not included them in our discussion.

The fabric used in batik may not be a blend—it must be 100-percent wool or cotton or silk, simply because the dyes are specific for certain fibers and will not take sufficiently on a blend. Although this does not sound like a problem (after all, you *can* find pure silks, wools, and cottons), it actually does present certain difficulties. In this age of modern technology, much of what is on the market as "cotton" or "silk" is not, in fact, pure cotton or silk. Take, for example, what is commonly called China silk; today it is at least 50-percent synthetic and is still called China silk. Many—probably most—cottons are really synthetic/cotton blends. There are also many wool/synthetic blends; but in our experience wool fabrics are much more carefully labeled as to their fiber content. The problem of blends is further compounded by the fact that many fabric salesmen do not themselves know the fiber content of the fabric they are selling and may sell you a blend inadvertently. So you really must be on guard when shopping for your fabric.

We offer some advice on the basis of much experience: First, stress to the salesman that you must have 100-percent silk or 100-percent cotton or 100-percent wool and explain to him why—you are going to dye the fabric yourself and the dyes work only on pure fibers. Second, check the label on the bolt yourself and see if there is any indication of fiber content. Third, if in doubt and if you have the time, take a swatch home first and test it before you buy it. Fourth, make sure the salesman writes "100-percent silk" or whatever on the receipt so that, if it turns out not to be, you have a chance of getting a refund.

In addition to its not being a blend, it is important that the fabric you use in batik *not* be treated in any way, i.e., made wrinkle-resistant or waterproof, finished, etc.

All of these treatments interfere with or even completely prevent the penetration of the fabric by the dye. When you buy your fabric, ask the salesman if it is drip-dry, wrinkle-resistant, finished, etc. He will be all too happy to tell you if it is—usually these treatments make the cloth more saleable. The problem of treated fibers is more common with cotton than with silk or wool, so be on guard particularly when shopping for cotton.

The fabric you select for batik must be either white or a pale color since you will be dyeing the cloth (several times, most likely) and changing the color. Remember, you can't obtain a light color over a dark color.

Even though you are largely limited to an unblended, untreated natural fiber when you do batik, there are many choices available to you. The first obviously is the choice of fiber: will you choose silk, wool, or cotton? And what *type* of wool, silk, or cotton will you choose?

Although there are no fast rules about the selection of fabric for batik, there are some considerations in making your decision.

CRITERIA FOR SELECTING FABRIC

In choosing your fabric, first consider the function of the batik you are going to make. What will the batik be used for? Will it be used for clothing—a skirt, dress, blouse? Will it be a decorative piece for the wall? Will it be for the house—a pillow, a curtain, a table runner? Such questions will help to isolate the type and weight of fabric most suitable for your work. For example, if you wish to make a blouse, a lightweight cotton might be most suitable. For a wall hanging you might choose a heavyweight silk that hangs well, has some texture, and takes color vividly. For a curtain you would probably choose a lightweight cotton like organdy because cotton dyes are less sensitive to light and the cotton can be washed. The more "practical" the fabric must be because of its ultimate function, the more likely you will be to choose cotton or wool.

Another factor in your choice of fabric is the color and texture effect you desire. Silks generally dye more intensely and vibrantly than cottons; wool also dyes intensely, but instead of the sheen inherent in many silks, wool has a definite, frequently nubby texture. Silks come in many textures: raw silk is nubby without sheen; China silk, surah, shantung, Thai silk have high sheens. Cottons are dull-finished, but there is textural variety among them: sailcloth and Indian Head have a definite weave, muslin has a rough finish, velveteen has a soft, pile finish. In order to obtain the color intensity and textural surface you desire, you must choose the fabric that will make this possible.

The choice of fabric will also depend upon the design you will apply to it. Will it be a bold or intricate design? It is more difficult to create an intricate design on heavyweight fabrics such as heavy wools, raw silks, or velveteen; therefore you should choose a lightweight fabric such as batiste, broadcloth, China silk, surah, or even chiffon. Some textural or translucent fabrics enhance certain designs but take away from others. Sometimes you will want a subtle, understated effect; for this you might choose an untextured cotton that will dye in softer shades.

We will now try to describe to you the various attributes of each type of natural fiber available, including their relative merits and disadvantages, and review the different forms of silk, cotton, and wool, which vary in weight, texture, sheen, durability, color absorbency, and washability.

SILK

Silk is truly a wonderful fabric. Its richness and its variety offer almost limitless possibilities in batik. Of its most significant attributes we would include first and foremost the intensity of color obtained when it is dyed —a fact true of all forms of 100-percent silk. A second characteristic is the wide choice it offers in terms of textures, weights, and sheens. Silks run from very heavy, textured or untextured raw silks, linen silks, or heavy-weight shantungs, to the very lightest and sheerest chiffons, from the high sheen of China silk to perfectly flat pongee silk. You can always find the right silk, in terms of weight, texture, translucence, and sheen, for whatever your purpose might be.

In addition silk has certain advantages in relation to the process of batik. First, it usually does not require prewashing before you begin to work. Most silk seems not to be sized or treated in ways that interfere with the dyeing process. Occasionally you may find natural oils present in the fabric, which means that the dye will be absorbed more slowly by the fabric, but the fabric will dye evenly and intensely in the end So with silk you can eliminate one step in the process, a step that, when you are working with many yards of fabric, may take up much time.

Second, except for the very heaviest of silks, the wax penetrates easily. Third, all of the lighter-weight silks dry quickly, which helps speed up the working process. Fourth, except for the very thick or heavily textured silks, it is possible to do intricate, finely detailed designs on silk. Even untextured raw silk allows much fine work with the *tjanting*.

Unfortunately there are some drawbacks to the use of silk in batik. Of prime consideration is the fact that silk cannot be machine-washed; it really should be dry-cleaned. For many purposes, therefore, it may not be desirable or practical. The inherent elegance of silk may present another design limitation: it tends to have a dressy look—something not always desirable. Furthermore, many silks are slippery and as a result may present difficulties when you are trying to stretch them on a frame; or the material may be extremely difficult to sew or work with after the batik is finished. A disadvantage with some silks, particularly China silk or chiffon, is their tendency to "run," especially when you tack them to the frame on which you work.

Another possible drawback to the use of silk is the fact that silk can be costly, and it is getting even costlier. These days silk will cost at least three dollars a yard and, more likely, five dollars or more. Especially when you are just beginning to do batik, you may be a little nervous about spending a lot of money without knowing what your result will be. However, with the cost of all fabrics rising daily—even cottons—the expense of silk does not seem to be so discouraging, especially when you *do see* the results.

In addition, we have found that 100-percent silk is becoming harder and harder to find, and while theoretically there is a tremendous variety in the types of silk produced (particularly in Japan and India), it may not be possible to find such a selection in the United States. Some fabric stores have old bolts of silks that they would gladly get rid of, but you must hunt around or persistently ask. It is sad but true that synthetics have all but replaced natural fibers and that the manufacturing of silk (as well as 100-percent cotton and 100-percent wool) is no longer profitable in this country.

Types of Silk
We can easily divide silks into heavyweight and light-weight.

Lightweight silks: In this category we would include silk chiffon, Georgette, crepe de chine, surah, China,

PLATE 3: *Long Chiffon Dress. Batik by Laura Adasko. Dress designed by Leaco.*

32

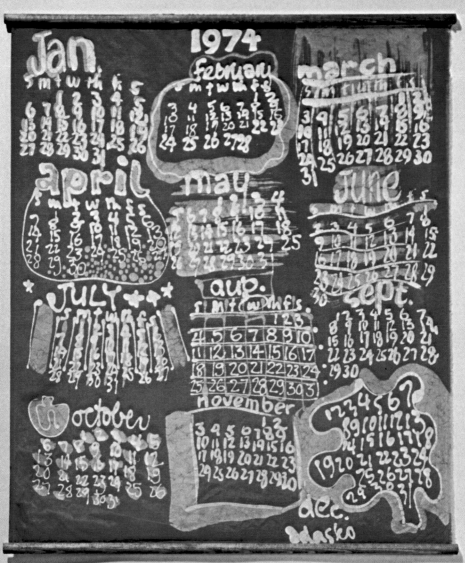

broadcloth, shantung, pongee. Silk chiffon and Georgette are transparent, very light and airy, soft to the touch, with a dull finish. They are particularly suitable for clothing but might also be used for curtains or for a room divider that light can come through. China silk and silk surah are opaque and shiny; they are most often used for scarves but would also be suitable for hangings; they are extremely slippery and are somewhat difficult to sew. Broadcloth and pongee are also opaque but have a dull finish and a close weave; they look like shirting material and, in fact, are most suitable for shirts and blouses, as well as other clothing. Pongee tends to be heavier than the broadcloth and the other lightweight silks and has more body; it might be a suitable fabric for men's ties or pillows or hangings or heavier-weight clothing that you don't want to line, such as kaftans or robes. All of these silks accept the dyes well.

Heavyweight silks: The silks in this category would include Thai silk, linen silks, heavy shantung, and raw silks (which come in many forms). Of all the silks, the raw silk takes the dye most intensely, but, because of its heavy weight and, in some cases, rich texture, its uses are limited. Raw silks are quite suitable for wall hangings, upholstery, pillows, and more tailored clothing. The raw silk has a quality of naturalness. In fact it doesn't really look like silk at all, particularly because of its dull, rough finish (sometimes it looks a bit like muslin or even suede). A drawback in working with raw silk is that it takes a long time to dry; also, it may be difficult for the wax to penetrate and thus might require rewaxing of the design. Linen silk is somewhat stiff (like linen) and could be used for table runners, tablecloths, or table

PLATE 4: *Batik Calendar and Books.*
Batiked and designed by Laura Adasko.
Calendar in China silk; book covers in
raw silk.

33

mats, as well as some clothing and hangings. Heavy shantung is suitable for some clothing, for hangings, pillows, and room dividers.

COTTON

The most outstanding characteristic of cotton is that it is extremely practical. It is washable by hand or machine, durable, and generally inexpensive, and it has a good colorfastness with most dyes. Like silk, cotton comes in a wide variety of weights and textures. You will always be able to find a cotton suitable for any purpose.

Cotton does have certain disadvantages, the most important being that cotton does not take color with the intensity or brilliance that wool and silk do. If color intensity is an important element in your particular batik, you would probably not choose a cotton to work on. Furthermore, cotton does not have the luster or richness of silk; it always has a dull finish. Of course, many times you will not want intensity of color or a high sheen in your work, and will choose to work on cotton.

Another disadvantage of cotton is that it is almost universally treated, either for sizing or for wrinkle resistance. These treatments interfere with the acceptance of the dye by the cloth and require that you wash the fabric thoroughly (perhaps several times) before working on it. This, of course, takes time, both in the washing and drying. Furthermore, it sometimes happens that the treatment is not completely or evenly removed, and the cloth will dye unevenly. It is even possible that washing will not remove the treatment at all. A good and rather ironic example of this is an experience we had when testing various dyes and cottons in preparation for writing this book. One fabric we tested, which we had been assured was 100-percent cotton voile, consistently refused to absorb the dye, even after it was washed. Whatever dye or color did appear was extremely pale and washed out.

We were very puzzled by this: it definitely felt like cotton and looked like cotton, and we had thought the salesman was reliable. Then we looked at all our cotton samples and noticed that, compared to the other cottons, the voile—after washing and dyeing—appeared wrinkle-free, almost as if it had been ironed. We concluded that this wrinkle-resistant fabric had been treated so well it had become undyeable and unusable for our purposes.

As we pointed out earlier, it has become increasingly more difficult to find 100-percent cotton, and this could present another difficulty in working with this fiber. Be sure to check for a label indicating fiber content before purchasing your fabric.

Types of Cotton
We also can divide cottons into lightweight and heavy-weight.

Lightweight cottons: This would include cotton batiste, organdy, broadcloth, poplin, bleached muslin, voile. Bleached muslin seems to dye consistently lighter than the other lightweight cottons (with the exception of voile, which seems to be treated and hence does not dye). It is a medium-weight, dull-finished, durable cotton which could be used for almost any purpose in batik; however, its inability to accept the dyes fully may be a drawback. Organdy dyes very beautifully, obtaining clear and strong color. This cotton would be highly suitable for curtains, or perhaps children's clothing, as it is translucent and light in weight. Organdy has a definite stiffness, almost a roughness, which might limit its uses. Batiste also dyes well, with a clarity and brilliance in color; it is a lightweight, opaque, close-weave and soft-textured fabric quite suitable for clothing, curtains, and perhaps wall hangings. All the lightweight cottons are easy to wax and dry quickly.

Heavyweight cottons: This category includes cotton sailcloth, Indian Head, unbleached muslin, and velveteen.

Sailcloth, Indian Head, and particularly the unbleached muslin consistently dye intensely and clearly. All of these cottons seem highly reliable in terms of color results. Unbleached muslin is medium or heavy in weight, slightly yellowish in color, with a natural rough finish, although still soft to the touch. It is an extremely practical fabric and could be used for all sorts of clothing or for decorative purposes without being flashy or frilly or fancy. Indian Head and sailcloth are heavier and stiffer than unbleached muslin, though still soft to the touch. Sailcloth has the look of canvas without its stiffness; it has a close weave that can be seen and which gives it a slight texture. It is a good fabric for hangings, interior decorating, pillows, and handbags, and for certain kinds of clothing such as pants and jackets. Indian Head is a bit lighter in weight than sailcloth; it looks like a linen without slubs, with a close weave and a slight stiffness. It could be used for hangings, table runners or mats, napkins, tablecloths, and some clothing.

Velveteen is 100-percent cotton, a heavyweight, soft-textured fabric with a distinctive nap or piled surface. When velveteen is dyed, the color appears more muted and subtle than on other cottons, but its texture gives it a rich and individual look. It is more difficult to wax than other cottons because of the pile, and it takes a long time to dry. Sometimes it requires waxing on both sides of the fabric because the wax does not sufficiently penetrate the cloth when applied to only one side and the design is lost. It is especially good for upholstery, pillows, hangings, and some clothing such as pants, long skirts, capes, or coats—it is particularly nice to use for something you will touch! Unlike most other cottons, it has a luxurious, dressy quality.

WOOL

Wool comes in many weights and textures, although in

comparison to cotton and silk it is generally heavier in weight. Wool has a distinctive flat finish and feel, but the texture and weave will vary greatly. Wool consistently dyes beautifully, as intensely as silk and more intensely than cotton. Obviously, it has many uses, particularly for clothing that requires a heavier, warmer fabric, such as suits, winter scarves, pants, jackets, capes, and dresses. It can also be used for hangings and coverings for beds or couches. Sometimes it is slightly irritating to the skin and may require lining. It is a durable, warm, and strong fabric.

Among the drawbacks in using wool is the fact that it is usually rather thick and it is sometimes difficult for the wax to penetrate the cloth sufficiently, requiring waxing on both sides of the fabric. In addition wool takes a very long time to dry. Also, we have found that wool tends to fade more easily than other fabrics. Wool has to be dry-cleaned, which is definitely a financial disadvantage. Furthermore, wool tends to be rather expensive today, costing as much as fifteen dollars a yard. Finally, it is sometimes as difficult to find 100-percent wool as it is to find 100-percent cotton, and you must look for labels to indicate fiber content. It may also be difficult to find white or light-colored, nonprinted 100-percent wool, because there is little demand for this kind of fabric.

Types of Wool
Among the many types of wool fabrics, some of the more common are wool challis, crepe, flannel, gabardine, and many kinds of knits. Of these types we are most familiar with wool challis since it is lightweight and easier to work with than the heavier wools. It is not necessary to wax both sides of wool challis as the wax will readily penetrate the cloth. Because of its lightness and the beauty of its drape, wool challis is extremely useful for clothing. It has a dull, flat, almost textureless look, although the weave is visible, and it is very soft to

the touch. Challis can be used for dresses, pants, shirts, hangings, lightweight jackets or coats or capes, and winter scarves.

OTHER POSSIBILITIES

In addition to those fabrics we have discussed, there are many more that may be of use to the batik craftsman. Some, such as linen or some wools, we have used from time to time, although our experience with them is limited. Others we have not yet experimented with, but they may be quite suitable, even exciting, to work with in batik. Such fabrics as corduroy, velour, terrycloth, burlap, or some more "exotic" silks such as silk organdy, silk brocade, even cotton suede or leather itself, might be quite effective for certain purposes and certain designs. Since we have not worked with them as yet, we do not feel competent to discuss or evaluate them. However, we really want to encourage you to experiment and explore all materials that are available and that might lend themselves to batiking. By constantly working and experimenting with new materials you will expand and enhance your knowledge and your skill. Each fabric you work with interacts with the batik medium in a different way, leading to different results and effects. Working with a silk chiffon is quite unlike working with velveteen, in every aspect of the batik process from designing to waxing to dyeing, and the feeling and the function of the work will also differ. In a sense, each new material will create a new vision, a new possibility for self-expression, self-development, and self-discovery, as well as an expansion of the medium itself.

Wax

Of all the methods of making designs on fabric, batik alone uses wax to create the design. Wax and the resulting crackle give batik its distinctive quality. The multicolored fine lines of batik are the result of the application of hot liquid wax to cloth. It is the wax that gives to batik the depth and texture that other processes of hand-designing fabrics can never capture. For a batik artisan, therefore, it is very important—and exciting—to learn about wax, its nature and eccentricities, and to see how its characteristics are cultivated in the batik process.

In batik wax is used in two states: as a hot liquid, about the consistency of a good brandy; and as a cold solid, like a candle or a crayon. When the wax is applied to the cloth, it is in its liquid form; once on the cloth it solidifies. In doing batik, you must become familiar with both states of the wax and learn how to take advantage of them.

HEATING THE WAX

To begin using the wax, you must first transform it from its solid to its liquid state by heating. There are two ways to heat wax which we consider safe and effective: by using an electric frying pan or by using a double boiler. The wax is heated to the point at which it flows smoothly from a brush and easily penetrates the fabric, thus forming a resist to the dye. This is the basic principle of batik: the wax creates a design by acting as a resist to dye wherever it is applied. Wax protects those areas of the cloth it covers by preventing the dye from penetrating. Essentially it is the *wax* that makes the design by covering some areas with wax and leaving others exposed to the dye.

If you are using an electric frying pan, which we prefer, simply place your wax in its solid form in the pan, turn the temperature control to 300–350 degrees, and let the wax melt. (You can leave tools in hardened wax.) You can find an inexpensive electric frying pan at most secondhand stores. You don't need a pan with a lid, because a lid is not necessary in heating the wax.

When the wax is liquified, test its flow on a scrap piece of fabric. If it penetrates (look at the reverse side of your swatch), you are ready to start your work.

Once the wax is heated to the proper consistency, the heat should be kept at a temperature that maintains the flow of the wax—about 325 degrees on an electric frying pan. Be very careful not to overheat the wax, because it is extremely explosive at high temperatures and can be very dangerous.

TOP: *Use either a double boiler or a frying pan for melting wax.*

BOTTOM: *Brushes and* tjantings *can be left in wax as it solidifies. Brushes will soften when the wax melts.*

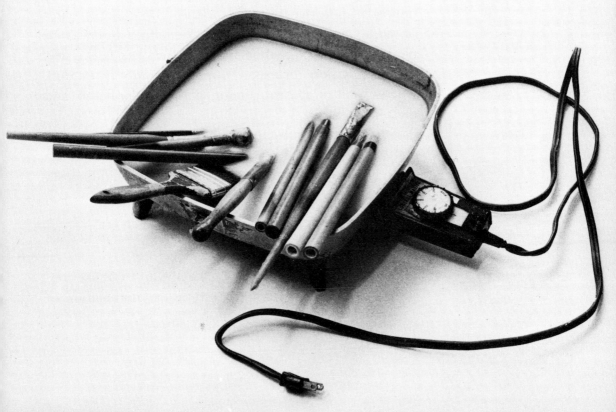

If you are using a double boiler, fill the bottom pan with water and place the solidified wax in the top pan. Turn your stove or hot plate to a moderately high temperature, until the water starts to boil and the wax starts to melt; then turn the temperature down so that the water continues to heat the wax without boiling away. Test the wax on a scrap to see if it penetrates sufficiently. With a double boiler the critical concern is to keep the boiling water at a high level so that it can continue to maintain the temperature of the wax. Check the water regularly, and add more when needed. If you hear a sizzling noise, it means you are low on water. It is helpful to have water nearby so that you can fill the bottom quickly and not interrupt your work.

Do not under any circumstances heat wax directly over an open flame. This is an unnecessary risk. If you do not have a double boiler or an electric frying pan, improvise a double boiler with an old pot and a tin can.

MIXTURE OF BEESWAX AND PARAFFIN

The temperature at which the wax will flow properly depends upon the type and/or the proportion of types of wax you use. In batik you use either beeswax or paraffin or a combination of both. Beeswax is the wax secreted by bees for making the honeycomb. It is a dull, yellow solid of agreeable odor, plastic when warm, and melting at about 143 to 151 degrees. Paraffin is an inflammable waxy substance, white in color, produced in distilling wood, shale, or coal, and occurring also in the earth as a constituent of petroleum or as a solid deposit. It melts at about 118 to 147 degrees. Therefore, if you use all or mostly paraffin, you will not have to heat the wax as much as you would beeswax in order to get the proper flow of wax.

But there are even more important and critical considerations in determining the type or combination of types of wax you use in your batik. Besides acting as a resist to dye when applied to cloth, the wax also *cracks*. When the wax cracks it creates many fine, veinlike lines, where the dye can seep in. This effect, the crackle, is the unique quality of batik.

Crackle creates texture, depth, shadow, movement, softness, tonality, richness, subtlety, vibration, energy, aliveness. It's hard to convey the specialness of crackle. It is the quality of batik that you can use or not use, which you can control but not control. It has a life of its own, it is independent and strong, yet it can be a partner in your creation as well. You and crackle work to create a batik. You are friends, and it is through your understanding of this friend that your batiks will grow and develop.

When you approach your batik, you will consider crackle in relation to your design. You might ask yourself, "How can I use crackle to enhance my design, to create the imagery I wish to create, the expression I wish to give?" How much crackle do I want? The more crackle you wish, the more paraffin you will use, because paraffin is more brittle than beeswax and cracks more readily. If you feel that a lot of crackle would take away from the feeling you wish to create, add more beeswax to your wax combination. But remember: the wax has a mind of its own and you can never *completely* control the amount of crackle you obtain. And this adds much life to the process of batik, because there is always the unexpected effect, the unknown result, the organic, dynamic relationship between you and the materials with which you work.

In trying to determine the amount of beeswax or paraffin you should use, we can offer a general suggestion:

Because paraffin is less expensive than beeswax and easily obtained at most hardware stores or supermarkets, use all or mostly paraffin (no more than 1 part beeswax to 4 parts paraffin) *unless:*

—you want very little crackle; or

—you are working on a large piece of fabric which must be crumpled inevitably while dyeing, thus cracking the wax a great deal; or

—you are working on a heavy cloth such as wool or heavy muslin which will also crumple while dyeing and from which paraffin seems to flake off easily; or

—you are going to dye your fabric many times, moving and crumpling each time you dye, which might create too much crackle in relation to your design; or

—your design is intricate and involves fine lines, which if broken would interfere with the overall effect you wish to create.

Beeswax is costly and somewhat difficult to obtain unless you live near a beekeeper. We have listed a few outlets in the List of Suppliers, page 151.

WAX TOOLS

Besides considering the combination of waxes you will use in making your batik, you need to give some thought to the tools you will use to apply the wax to the cloth. The brushes you use should be firm and thick enough to keep the wax hot. The best brushes we have found for batik are Oriental bamboo brushes, because, while they are thick enough to hold the wax, they are tapered to a point to allow fine-line work. They come in a wide selection of sizes, are reasonably priced, and if cared for will last a long time. Large household brushes can be used for bold designs or for filling in large areas of wax. Whatever brushes you use, consider them a gift to your craft— use them only for batik. It is impossible to remove the wax completely from a brush, and whatever else you might use them for could interfere with your batik.

OPPOSITE: *Create "crackle" before dyeing.*

45

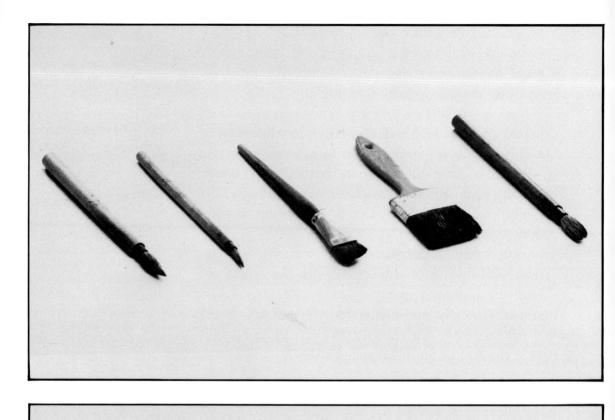

In addition to brushes, a traditional Indonesian batik tool which you can also use is the *tjanting*. A *tjanting* is used to create fine lines and intricate details or designs. It is a small metal cup with a spout attached to a wooden handle. The cup is placed in the wax pot, filled with wax, and then applied to the cloth, the wax flowing out through the spout. The *tjanting* comes with variously sized spouts to form lines ranging from very thin to medium, and it also comes with multispouts. *Tjantings* can be obtained at some art-supply stores and batik suppliers. We include a list of places where you can get them in the List of Suppliers, page 151.

REMOVAL OF WAX

After your batik is dyed, the wax must be removed from the cloth. This is a very exciting point in the process for it is at this moment, after many applications of wax and many dyebaths, that the total design is revealed. Until this time your batik has remained a mystery because the wax covering the various dyes in your batik has distorted and muted their intensity. At last you see the true colors and the effect of crackle.

The Iron-Out Method

There are several methods of removing wax. One way is to iron out the wax with an iron, by placing the batik between newsprint or newspaper and pressing with a fairly hot iron. This iron-out method is most suitable when you are 1) working on a small piece of cloth and won't have to press yards of fabric; or 2) working on lightweight cloth which absorbs less wax; or 3) planning to dip the fabric in a chemical solvent but you want to

Top LEFT: *Several kinds of brushes used for batik.*

BOTTOM: *Batik* tjantings.

47

remove some of the wax to facilitate the action of the chemical; or finally 4) working on a piece from which complete wax removal is not required, such as a small hanging. With this method the wax is never *completely* removed, and some stiffness remains in the cloth. It is a prelude to the application of other techniques of wax removal that will complete the wax-removal job.

To use the iron-out method, place newspaper on an ironing board or table, place the batik fabric on top of it, and then cover the batik with more newspaper. Now apply a hot iron to the covered batik. As you press, the newspaper will absorb the wax. You will see the wax penetrating the paper, leaving an oil-like image of your design. As the newspaper fills up with wax, change both the bottom and top layers of paper and press again. This time less wax will appear on the newspaper. Continue this process until little or no wax can be seen on the newspaper. Now look at the batik. Sometimes you will see a dark outline around your design which is the result of an oily wax residue. If this hinders your design, use an additional wax-removal technique.

Don't apply your iron directly to the waxed batik, as the wax will melt and collect on both your iron and your ironing board, ruining both. You must always have something—preferably newsprint or newspaper—which will absorb the wax. You may press the fabric directly once you've completed the iron-out method.

Sometimes you will find that the newsprint from newspaper will come off on your cloth as you press it, although generally this will not happen. If you are concerned about possible transference of ink to your cloth, use paper towels, paper bags, or newsprint bought at art-supply stores for ironing out wax.

PLATE 5: *Scarves. Batiks by both authors.*
Top row in silk chiffon; bottom row in
China silk.

48

LEFT: *Working on an ironing board or table, place the waxed batik on top of a piece of newspaper.*

RIGHT: *Cover the batik with a second piece of newspaper.*

PLATE 6: *Wrap Wool Dress. Batik by Alice Huberman; sewn by Marilyn Wilson. China Silk Scarf. Batik by Laura Adasko.*

LEFT: *As you press, the newspaper will absorb the wax.*

RIGHT: *Continue pressing until no wax appears on the paper, then look at the batik.*

Removal with Chemical Solvents

A second method for removing wax is the application of chemical solvents such as benzene or carbon-tetrachloride, which can be obtained at most hardware stores. These fluids are extremely effective in dissolving and removing the wax; benzene, however, is highly inflammable and the fumes of both are unhealthy. They are also somewhat expensive. Use chemical solvents when you want to remove the wax completely such as for fabric for clothing which should not be stiff. Often chemical solvents can be used in conjunction with the iron-out method. Remove most of the wax with the iron, and then remove the remaining wax with the solvent.

Using solvents is very unpleasant; they have a strong, disagreeable odor; their fumes are extremely unhealthy and may cause dizziness or even headaches; and, as we said before, benzene is inflammable. Therefore it is extremely important that you use these solvents only in places with good ventilation, preferably out of doors.

Because of the dangers of using these chemicals, we do not recommend using them when removing wax from large pieces of fabric, since this would require an excessive amount of solvent. It is best to have large pieces professionally dry-cleaned. For smaller pieces we strongly suggest that you iron out most of the wax first so that you minimize the amount of solvent you must use and the amount of time it takes to apply it. Reserve the use of solvents for small batiks or for pieces from which complete wax removal is desired.

When using these solvents, pour enough to barely cover the fabric into a plastic or enamel basin. Put rubber gloves on (a special pair you use *only* for wax removal). Now submerge the cloth in the solvent bath. Move the cloth around, allowing it to soak in the solvent. When the solvent starts to thicken (it begins to become opaque and gray in color), pour it out and fill the bath with fresh solvent. Submerge the cloth again, and repeat this process as many times as it takes to remove the wax completely from the cloth. Hang the fabric to dry; the odor of the solvent should disappear when the solvent has evaporated.

The Boil-Out Method

A third way to remove wax is called the boil-out method. To remove the wax, dip the cloth in boiling water several times. Each time more and more of the wax will melt and rise to the top of the pot, until all the wax is removed. An advantage of this technique is that you can collect the wax and reuse it. A possible disadvantage is that you may lose some of your color by submerging your batik in boiling water. This, of course, depends on the fastness of the dyes you are using. Boiling also may weaken the fibers of your cloth.

Wax, and the resulting crackle, are the elements that make batik different from any other form of fabric decoration. Understanding the properties of wax and how they work, as well as learning the techniques of applying wax to cloth so that you, the artist, feel in control, takes time and practice. Yet, as we have said, simply working toward this point is not only rewarding, it is fun! You will learn from your "mistakes"—and, as you learn, you will almost assuredly produce designs and fabrics you will love and cherish.

Dyes

Since it is by the use of dyes that color is introduced to the batik medium, dyes are a central part of the craft. Color is created in the process of dyeing, and color gives life to the batik design. So it is essential that anyone pursuing batik learn about dyes and how to use them.

At first dyes may appear a bit intimidating because they are chemicals and because they require a certain exactness and control to achieve reliable results. However, once you are familiar with the basic procedure, the process comes easily. Once you have a certain sense of the basic steps and proportions and the different characteristics of the various dyes, once you've experimented with several dyes and experienced the results, you will be able to select intelligently the dyes best suited for your work, and you will be able to carry out the steps of the dyeing process without a second thought.

GENERAL CONSIDERATIONS
OF BATIK DYEING

There are certain characteristics of batik dyeing that define and limit the choice of dyes and the process of dyeing itself. First, batik requires the use of cold-water dyes, because batik involves the application of wax to create a design. If the waxed cloth is placed into a dye-bath with a temperature greater than 110 degrees, the wax will start to melt and break off, and your design will be lost. So you are limited to a dye that will adhere in temperatures around 90 to 110 degrees Fahrenheit, depending upon your wax mixture. This is a critical limitation, since most manufactured dyes require high temperatures and often long periods of boiling to be effective. However, there are certain cold-water dyes available for batik which we will discuss and evaluate in this chapter.

The type of dye you will use and the procedure used in dyeing depend upon the type of *fiber* of the fabric you have chosen to dye. Generally there are three types of dyes available to the batik craftsman: reactive dyes, direct dyes, and acid dyes. *Reactive dyes* can be used on cotton, linen, silk, and wool, and with all these fibers the procedure is the same. These dyes require the use of both salt and washing soda in the dyeing process. *Direct dyes* are used only for cotton and linen, and they require the use of salt as an assistant in the dyeing process. *Acid dyes* are used for dyeing silk and wool and require the use of acetic acid in the dyeing process.

In addition to these three general types, *household dyes* (designed for high-temperature dyeing) can also be used, but since they must be used at cool temperatures in batik their color effectiveness is greatly reduced. Other dyes that have been suggested for batik use are *vat dyes,*

OPPOSITE: *Several types of batik dyes.*

suitable for cotton, linen, and silk, and *naphthol dyes,* suitable only for cotton or linen.

Since dyes determine the color achieved in your batik, the *intensity* of color depends upon the dye you choose to work with, the amount of dyestuff used, how much water is used in proportion to the dye, the length of time the cloth is immersed in dye, and finally, how much fabric is to be dyed. Each dye, of course, has its own procedure and idiosyncrasies as to amount of.dyestuff used, length of time for dyeing, and assistants added to facilitate the dye. However, there are a few general principles to keep in mind when you are considering the intensity of color you wish to achieve:

1. Generally, the more dyestuff you use, the more intense the color will be.
2. The more water you add to the dyebath, the less intense the color will be.
3. The longer the cloth remains in the dyebath, the more intense the color will be.
4. The size and weight of the fabric to be dyed will determine the amount of the dyebath. The larger and heavier the fabric, the larger the dyebath will be. The larger and heavier the fabric, the more dyestuff you will use, the more water you will add to it, and the larger the container in which you dye the fabric will have to be.
5. The cloth when wet will look quite a bit darker than the actual color will be when the cloth is dry. Although there is no absolute rule, we can say that the cloth should appear roughly to be twice as intense when wet as you want it to be when dry.

BASIC EQUIPMENT FOR BATIK DYEING

No matter which dyes you choose to work with, they will all require the same equipment in the process of dyeing. First, you will need *basins* or *containers* for the dyebath itself. These must be made of plastic, stainless steel, or enamel, materials which will not interact or absorb the dye. Second, you will need a glass or stainless steel *measuring cup*, plastic *measuring spoons*, and a stainless *spoon* for stirring the dyes. Third, you will need a *kettle* to boil water in, in order to dissolve the dyestuff. A pair of *rubber gloves* will also be necessary to protect your hands from the dyes. The dyes are absorbed easily by the skin and could be dangerous to your health, so you should get into the habit of wearing gloves as you work with the dyes. We suggest that you buy a sturdy type of rubber glove, as many gloves designed for household use are somewhat flimsy and have a tendency to tear. You will also need a *container* in which to rinse your fabric after it is dyed. For rinsing you could use another plastic or enamel basin or a sink or bathtub. Be sure to wash it out after use to remove any particles of dye possibly remaining. Finally, you will need a place to hang your batik to dry. A *clothesline* with *clothespins* or a *clothes rack* designed for drying hand washing would be suitable.

The utensils selected for batik dyeing should be used exclusively for that purpose, since the dyes are chemicals and are hazardous if ingested or absorbed by the body. If you use a sink or bathtub for rinsing, be sure to clean it thoroughly. Do not use your dye measuring spoons or cups for food preparation. Do not use your basins or your gloves for the family wash. This is not only a precautionary measure. The separation of your batik equipment from other aspects of your life will help you organize and simplify your method of working, making it easier ultimately for you to do the work.

THE DYEING PROCEDURE—STEP BY STEP

Each type of dye will have its own basic formula and dyeing procedure, which we will describe when con-

A bathtub can be a useful utensil for rinsing batik. Special rubber gloves, used only for batik, are essential.

sidering and evaluating the types of dyes available for batik. But regardless of the type of dye you choose to work with, there is a general procedure for dyeing. It is helpful to become familiar with all the steps of the dyeing process before starting your work so that you can be prepared for all aspects of batik dyeing. Furthermore, such a review of the dyeing procedure, step by step, will be helpful in avoiding mistakes and achieving the effects that you desire.

Step 1: Wetting the Cloth

The first step in the dyeing process is to wet the cloth thoroughly in a bath of cold water. (Remember to use cold water; hot water may destroy your wax design.) This wetting of the fabric is essential because it enables the cloth to absorb the dye thoroughly. It may take longer for some fabrics to become wet, particularly heavier silks or wool; simply leave them in the water for a longer period of time before dyeing. It will be obvious when the cloth is totally wetted because the fibers will look different.

After the cloth is wet, it is advisable to hang the fabric for a few minutes or to hold the fabric above the water to allow the excess water to run off the cloth, because any water contained in the fabric will be added to the dyebath, weakening the dye's intensity. Allowing the excess water to drain off the fabric will also make it easier to handle, especially with the heavy fabrics, as the water makes the fabric heavier.

Step 2: Mixing the Dye

The dyes can be mixed while the fabric is soaking in water or hanging to drain off excess water, or you may wish to mix the dyes before wetting the fabric. The way in which the dye is mixed and dissolved and the assistants added to it depend upon the dye type, and you must follow the instructions printed on the package of each specific dye. It is at this stage that you will decide how strong a color you wish, for the intensity of the color is partly the result of the proportion of dyestuff to water.

First, dissolve the dye powder with hot or cold water according to specific instructions for the dye you are using. Be sure all the dye particles are dissolved. If they are not, you might spot your cloth and spoil your design. Once the dye is dissolved, pour it into a dye basin and add cold water to it, the amount to be determined by the amount of cloth to be dyed and the intensity of color you desire. Stir the bath so that water and dye become combined.

Step 3: Testing the Temperature
At this point, check the temperature of your bath. Some people use a thermometer to check the temperature though we rely on a more simple (and less accurate) method of sticking our finger briefly into the dyebath. If it feels no warmer than lukewarm, it is cool enough to use. If it feels warmer than lukewarm, we add a little cold water or wait until it cools. Keep in mind that any water added to the bath weakens the color.

The temperature of the dyebath should be within the range of 90 to 110 degrees. If the dyebath is hotter than 110 degrees, the wax will start to melt and the design will be lost. However, it is also true that the higher the temperature is, the more effective the dyes will be. So it is important to keep the bath as warm as possible without losing the wax design.

Step 4: Testing the Color
Before dyeing your waxed fabric, test the dyebath for color. Cut a small swatch of the fabric you are about to dye, wet it, and place it in the dyebath. After a few minutes take it out and see what color you have obtained. If it is darker than you want, add more water to the bath. If it is much weaker than you want (remember

that you haven't left it in the bath for the required length of time, so of course it will appear somewhat lighter than what the result will actually be), mix more dye and add it to the dyebath. The fabric will be twice as dark when wet than when dried.

Step 5: Adding Soap
Adding a little mild liquid soap, such as Lux or Ivory, to your dyebath may facilitate even dyeing. It actually makes a discernible difference with some dyes; experiment to find out if it is helpful with the dyes you are using.

Step 6: Adding the Assistant
The last step before actually dyeing is the addition to the dyebath of whatever assistant is required, usually either acid or salt. Add the assistant just before your cloth is placed in the dye, as the effect of the assistant in aiding the penetration of the dye will be lessened if it interacts with the dye for a long period of time. The amount and type of assistant to be added depends upon the dye used; check your specific dye instructions.

Step 7: Dyeing the Cloth
The dyebath is now ready, but before submerging the cloth in the bath, put on rubber gloves.

Submerge the cloth quickly and all at once, if possible. Move the cloth around until it is completely covered with dye. Continue to stir according to the instructions of the dye you are using. If you are dyeing a big piece of cloth, you will probably have to keep the cloth moving so that all parts are dyed with equal intensity. Remember to add any additional chemicals or assistants if they are required.

When the cloth has dyed to the intensity you desire or for the length of time indicated by the directions, remove the cloth from the dyebath.

Step 8: Rinsing the Cloth

After the cloth is dyed, place it in a bath of clean, cool water. A bathtub, sink, or basin can be used. The cloth should be moved around in the water to allow any excess dye to run out into the rinse water. Drain the first rinse water and add clean water. This process of rinsing and draining should continue until no more dye comes off the cloth. After you have finished rinsing, do *not* wring the cloth or crumple it in any way, as this would crack the wax and interfere with your design. To drain off as much water as possible, let your fabric remain in the tub or basin for a while after the water has been drained or else hold the cloth above the tub to let excess water run off the cloth.

Step 9: Hanging the Cloth to Dry

Now hang the cloth to dry inside or outside, using a clothesline and clothespins or special laundry racks. Use plastic clothespins, since wood clothespins will absorb the dye from the cloth and may possibly spot your work when you use them again. If you hang your cloth inside the house, you may want to place newspaper or plastic underneath the cloth or hang it over a bathtub or sink, since the cloth will lose much colored liquid in the drying process.

If possible, hang your cloth flat, stretched to its full width and not folded over your clothesline. This will make the cloth easier to restretch and work on again as well as preventing dye from accumulating in folds and spotting your batik.

Step 10: Storing Your Dyebaths and Dyes

Once the cloth is dyed, you may want to store the dye-

Top left: *Batik dyes, soaps and assistants.*

Bottom: *Dye the cloth in a small basin. Remember to wear rubber gloves. Submerge the cloth quickly and evenly.*

After the cloth is dyed, rinse it in a bath of clean, cool water.

PLATE 7: *Kimono. Batik on pongee silk by Alice Huberman. Loaned by Leslie Rankow, New York.*

*After rinsing, let the water drip off the cloth. Wringing will create
additional, perhaps unwanted, crackle.*

PLATE 8: *Shawl and Accessories. Shawl
in silk pongee, batiked and hand-fringed
by Alice Huberman. Purses and Belt.
Batiks by both authors; appliquéd by
Tamala Design, New York.*

bath for reuse. With many of the dyes available for batik, this is not possible at all, or for only a short time, since after any assistant is added to a dyebath its potency diminishes rapidly. You can experiment, of course, and see if it is possible to reuse your dyes and get effective colors. Remember that any dye will be less effective the second or third time it is used, since each time a piece is dyed it absorbs color from the bath, reducing its intensity.

If you wish to store dyes, glass or plastic bottles are preferable. Use a funnel to transfer the dye from the basin to the bottle. Sometimes refrigeration helps to maintain the potency of dyes. Or you can store your bottles on shelves or in boxes, labeling them carefully as to color and date of first use. If, after some days, algae form in the stored dyes or the dye precipitates out of the water and will not remix, throw the dye away, because it is then unusable.

Unmixed dyes, i.e., dyes in powder form, can be stored forever as they will not deteriorate unless mixed. Some dyes will cake up and clump if kept in a moist place or if not sealed off from air. Keep your jars or packets of dye in a dry place, lids tightly shut, preferably away from any water sources such as sinks or bathtubs—in which they might fall!

Step 11: Fixing the Dye
Once the batik is completed and the wax has been removed, it may be necessary or preferable to fix the color. Whether fixing is required depends upon the type of dye and how necessary it is for the piece to be colorfast. Again, check the package instructions and consider the function of your batik.

Color is fixed by heat. In most dyeing processes, the color is fixed in the process itself because the cloth is dyed at high temperatures. However, in batik the heat must be applied *after* the cloth is dyed since heat during the dyeing process would destroy the design. There are two methods of fixing the color by heat: ironing the cloth or steaming the cloth. Ironing is by far the simplest and in most cases a perfectly adequate method. After the cloth is dyed and the wax removed, the cloth is ironed at a temperature appropriate for its particular fiber. Steaming is a rather more complicated process and is not required with any of the batik dyes, except when the dye is painted directly onto the fabric (as described in Color, page 96).

If you do wish to steam the cloth to ensure fixing or if you have painted with the dyes instead of dyeing by immersion, there are several possible ways to steam your fabric:

> *Making your own steamer:* It is possible to make a steamer by using a large pot or even a metal garbage can. You will need a burner or electric hot plate; a pot or a garbage can; a homemade wire basket that fits inside the pot, not touching the sides and about 6 inches from the bottom of the pot, which can hook at the top, *or* a platform such as a milk-bottle rack that can be placed on the bottom of the pot and is at least 6 inches from the bottom. To use the steamer, put about 2 inches of water in the pot and place the pot on a stove or electric burner. Place newspaper, paper towels, or lightweight cloth on the fabric to be steamed so that all the cloth is covered. Then, roll the fabric so that none of the fabric touches itself. Wrap the roll of cloth completely with paper or cloth and then fold it only enough to fit into the steamer. Wrap the bundle again completely with a piece of felt cloth. Place another piece of felt and more newspaper on the bottom of the basket or on the top of the platform. Carefully fit the wrapped fabric into the basket or onto the platform, being sure that it does not touch

any part of the steamer. Cover at the top with more newspaper, extending over the sides of the pot. Put a lid on top of the newspaper and steam the fabric for 5 to 30 minutes, depending upon the amount and type of fabric.

Baking in an oven: You may dry- or steam-bake fabric in your oven. Again, wrap and roll fabric in the same way as you would for the steamer, making sure that the fabric does not touch itself. Place a pan of hot water on the bottom shelf of the oven. Place the wrapped fabric on the top shelf and bake at 285 to 300 degrees for 15 to 30 minutes.

Using a sauna: If you have a sauna or access to one, this is the simplest method for steaming fabric. Roll your fabric with newspaper, paper towels, or cloth, insert the roll into a cardboard tube, and then wrap the tube in a piece of felt. Set the sauna for 250 degrees and bake the cloth for 15 to 30 minutes.

Using a steam iron: Iron your fabric for at least five minutes with a steam iron set at 285 degrees.

Although the steaming process may appear complicated, once the equipment has been set up and you are familiar with the technique, it really is quite simple. Furthermore, *in most cases of batik dyeing, steaming is not necessary.* In fact, some dyes available for batik do not require any method for fixing the dyes, ironing or steaming. And even if the dye you are using recommends ironing or steaming to fix it, it may not be necessary in your particular case, since colorfastness may not be a critical concern for the particular project you are working on.

BATIK DYES AND HOW TO USE THEM

The major types of dyes available for batik are the fiber-reactive dyes, the direct dyes, the acid dyes, and Sennelier dyes (a French dye whose chemical classification is undetermined). Each dye type has its own particular dye formula and dyeing procedure.

Fiber-Reactive Dyes

The fiber-reactive dyes can be used on cotton, linen, silk, wool, and viscose rayon. Although there are many brands available in the United States, the most familiar and available seem to be Pylam, Fibrec, Hi Dye, and Dylon. All fiber-reactive dyes use the same basic formula and procedure.

Fiber-reactive dyes were first produced in England by ICI Organics in 1956. The trade name of the fiber-reactive dyes for cold-water dyeing is the Procion M series. Fiber-reactive dyes are distinguished from other dyes by the fact that the dye molecule forms a bond with the fiber itself. This means that these dyes are extremely reliable in terms of permanency and sensitivity to light and washing.

Fiber-reactive dyes require the use of two assistants in the dyeing process: salt and washing soda. The salt assists the dye's penetration into the fiber, while the washing soda helps to fix the dye. The amount of salt and dye powder used in the dyeing process depends upon the amount and weight of cloth to be dyed and the intensity of color desired. The basic formula is as follows:

For One Pound of Fabric
(approximately 3 yards average-weight fabric)

Intensity of Color	Amount of Dye	Amount of Water	Amount of Salt	Amount of Washing Soda
Light	¼ teasp.	2½ gal.	3 tablesp.	2 tablesp.
Medium	½ teasp.	2½ gal.	6 tablesp.	2 tablesp.
Dark	1 teasp.	2½ gal.	9 or more tablesp.	2 tablesp.

For heavier fabric or greater yardage, the amount of dye powder, salt, and water will of course increase. Also, if you do not achieve the intensity of color you desire, even using 1 teaspoon of dye, increase the quantity of dye powder, always remembering, to increase the amount of salt in the proper proportion.

The basic method in using fiber-reactive dyes is as follows:

1. Mix the dye powder with a little cold water in your measuring cup to the consistency of paste, then add up to 1 cup hot (not boiling) water, stirring the dye until it is completely dissolved.
2. Pour the dye concentrate into the dye basin and add the appropriate amount of water.
3. Wet your fabric and, just before submerging the fabric in the dyebath, add the appropriate quantity of salt to your bath.
4. Submerge the cloth in the dye. Keep the fabric constantly moving in the dyebath for 10 minutes while avoiding too much crackle.
5. Dissolve washing soda or fixer (some brands come with fixer). Dye the cloth for an additional 15 minutes, stirring occasionally.
6. Remove and rinse. When no excess dye appears in the rinse water, hang the cloth to dry.
7. No fixing process is necessary with the fiber-reactive dyes.

Direct Dyes

Direct dyes can be used on cotton, linen, and viscose rayon; some of the more common brand names are Craftool, Miyako, Aljo, and Fezan. Although the amount of dye used and the length of time required in the dyeing will vary from brand to brand, the basic formula for mixing and the basic procedure for dyeing remain the same.

Salt as an assistant is added in the ratio of 1 teaspoon per quart of prepared dye. Thus 2½ gallons of water—the standard size of a dyebath for 1 pound (3 yards) of cloth—would require the addition of 3 tablespoons of salt.

The basic procedure for using direct dyes is as follows:

1. Dissolve the dye in a little *hot* water; then add cold water.
2. The amount of dyestuff used depends upon the intensity of color desired and the quantity of cloth to be dyed. Experiment until you know what amounts will yield different intensities.
3. Pour dissolved dye concentrate into a basin; add the necessary amount of water to cover the cloth.
4. Wet the cloth and, just before submerging it in the bath, add the required amount of salt and stir.
5. Submerge the cloth in the dyebath and stir occasionally until the cloth is dyed to the desired intensity (from 20 minutes to an hour).
6. Remove cloth from dye; rinse and hang to dry.
7. Ironing may be useful in fixing the dye.

Acid Dyes
Acid dyes can be used for silk or wool; well-known brand names are Aljo, Craftool, Fezan, and Aiko. All acid dyes require the use of acetic acid as an assistant in the dyeing process. Acetic acid can be obtained from drugstores, chemical-supply houses, or photographic-supply houses (glacial acetic acid). The acid used should be diluted in water to 30 percent, although sometimes you can buy it already diluted to your specifications.

If you cannot obtain acetic acid, white vinegar can be substituted, but since vinegar is only about 5 percent acetic acid you have to use a correspondingly greater amount of vinegar in the dyeing process.

Formulas for acid dyes vary from brand to brand. The

amount of dye used and the length of time the cloth is in the dyebath will determine the intensity of color achieved. In general, for every teaspoon of dyestuff used, one teaspoon of acetic acid (30 percent) or two table-spoons of white vinegar are added.

Basically the procedure in using acid dyes is as follows:

1. Make a paste by mixing dyestuff with a little cold water; then add 1 pint hot water and heat the dye until it boils. Let the dye cool.
2. Pour the dye concentrate into a basin and add the required amount of water. Wet the cloth to be dyed.
3. Just before dyeing the cloth, add the appropriate amount of acetic acid or vinegar to the dyebath, stir the bath, and then submerge the cloth.
4. Dye the cloth, stirring occasionally, until the de-sired intensity of color is obtained.
5. Remove cloth from bath, rinse, and hang to dry.
6. Steaming is recommended to fix the dye to the fabric, but ironing can also be used.

PLATE 9: *Detail of Batik. Design by Laura Adasko on silk broadcloth.*

PLATE 10: *Blouses. Clockwise from top left: Silk Chiffon Blouse. Batik by Laura Adasko; blouse designed by Valerie Porr, New York. Cap-sleeve Blouse in silk broadcloth. Batik by Laura Adasko; blouse designed by Tamala Design, New York. Wrap Blouse in silk chiffon. Batik by both authors; blouse designed by Leaco. Man's Shirt in silk broadcloth. Batik by Alice Huberman; shirt designed by Tamala Design, New York.*

Sennelier Dyes

Another dye available for batik is known as Sennelier, a French dye available at a few stores in this country. Since we have not been able to find out its chemical type, and the procedure in using this dye is different from that of the other three types, we have put it in its own special category.

Sennelier dye can be used on silk, linen, cotton, or wool, although the dyes take with greater intensity on silk or wool and its reliability on cotton is not known. This dye requires no assistant in the dyeing process. Color intensity depends upon the amount of dyestuff used and the length of time the cloth is dyed.

Sennelier dyes require the following procedures:

1. Dissolve the dyestuff in a little boiling water; then add enough cold water to make 1 cup.
2. Pour the dye concentrate into a dye basin; add the required amount of water for the quantity of fabric to be dyed.
3. Wet the cloth and submerge in the dyebath. Stir and move the fabric around as it dyes.
4. When the cloth is dyed to the desired shade, remove from the bath and rinse.
5. Hang the cloth to dry. There are no recommended fixing procedures.

Other Dyes

In addition to the dyes we have already described, which

PLATE 11: *Long Dress in Silk Crepe. Batik by Alice Huberman. Dress designed and sewn by Marilyn Wilson.*

PLATE 12: *Pants Suit in Raw Silk. Batik by Alice Huberman; sewn by Marilyn Wilson. Silk Chiffon Scarf. Batik by Laura Adasko.*

are the most common batik dyes, there are a few other types of dyes which may be used for batik.

First, there are the *common household dyes,* such as Rit. However, when used at low temperatures they are not as reliable in terms of colorfastness or effective in terms of color intensity. If you try these dyes, follow the instructions on the package, but remember to reduce the dyebath temperature to around 100 degrees before dyeing the fabric.

Vat dyes such as Inkodye can also be used for batik on silk, cotton, linen, and viscose rayon. The most distinctive feature of these dyes is that they are pigments, not actually dyes, which, through the addition of various chemicals during the dyeing process, are converted into dyes. Moreover, the color does not appear as a result of the dyeing process but is developed by the exposure of the cloth to sunlight. These dyes are recommended for their colorfastness. Although the method will vary somewhat with the kind of vat dye used, the dyeing process involves first dyeing the cloth, then hanging it wet in the sun until the color develops, and finally, fixing the dye by ironing.

Naphthol dyes are another type of dye which may have application to the batik medium. They can be used only on cotton and linen and require a number of chemicals in the process of dyeing. These dyes are not carried in retail stores and must be obtained directly from the manufacturers, who do not recommend them for home use.

A REVIEW AND EVALUATION
OF BATIK DYES

For this book we thought it would be helpful to review and test the various dyes available for batik. We were particularly interested in comparing dyes in terms of color intensity, availability, price, simplicity of use, and reliability. We tested primary colors of all the brands we could obtain—a red, a yellow, and a blue. In order to test color intensity, we used the same quantity of dye and water in each bath: 1 teaspoon dyestuff to 1 quart water. This is a very high concentrate and even the weakest dye should give some color result. In each dyebath we tested five types of silk, seven types of cotton, and one type of wool. With each dye we followed the dyeing instructions specific to the type of dye, i.e., reactive, direct, or acid, and any special instructions for the particular brand.

In evaluating the dyes we used the following criteria:

First, we looked at color intensity. How strong was the dye? Did it give intense, clear color? Was the same color intensity obtained with cotton, wool, and silk, or was there variability depending on the type of fiber? Did all the color take with equal intensity—was the blue as strong as the yellow or red?

Second, we wanted to evaluate the dyes in terms of their practicality. We wanted to learn how expensive they were, how available they were, how easily they could be used as a result of brand packaging and particular brands' dyeing processes.

Finally, we also wanted to look at and evaluate the dyes in terms of colorfastness and method of fixing the dye, if such a method was required.

The dyes we tested were Pylam, Dylon, Fibrec, Craftool, Cushing, and Sennelier.

Pylam

Pylam is a fiber-reactive dye available in many colors. The average price per ounce is $1.00, but the manufacturer requires a minimum order of $15.00 plus shipping. These dyes are not available in retail art-supply stores and must be ordered directly from the manufacturer.

Pylam dyes gave a good color intensity on all the fabrics tested: wool, cotton, and silk. All three colors dyed to an equal intensity and seemed consistent on all the fibers tested.

The dyeing process is relatively simple, requiring the addition of salt and washing soda, and the dye mixes and dissolves easily. The bath must be stirred during the first half of the dyeing process, which in all takes about half an hour. Pylam dyes are sold in jars which are easy to use and to store. They have a high degree of color-fastness and require no special fixing process.

Dylon

Dylon dyes are fiber-reactive dyes manufactured in England by ICI Organics. They can be obtained at some art- or craft-supply stores in this country.

A distinct disadvantage of Dylon is its packaging. The dyes come in small round aluminum cans that must be punctured with a sharp object in order to let the dye out. Once the cans are opened they cannot be closed. The struggle to open the can inevitably gets dye over you and wastes quite a bit of it. Each can contains ½ ounce of dye and sells for about fifty cents.

The dyeing process is the same as with Pylam, requiring the use of salt and washing soda and about half an hour to complete the process. Stirring is necessary in the first half of the process. Sometimes Dylon is difficult to dissolve and tends to clump while being mixed.

Dylon gave good color intensity on cotton and wool but only fair color intensity on silk. Moreover, the colors were not consistently intense; the yellow was invariably weak, no matter which fiber was used. The blue and red were consistently deep in shade. Like other reactive dyes, Dylon does not require special fixing procedures, and it is considered highly colorfast.

Fibrec

Fibrec, another fiber-reactive dye, is available at retail art-supply stores in this country. It is sold in small plastic packets containing about ½ ounce of dyestuff and a small package of fixer (washing soda) for around $1.00. The packets must be cut to open and dye may come off on your scissors and hands, which is annoying as well as a waste of dye. The dyes, once opened, must be stored in other containers.

Fibrec gave a good color intensity and all three colors were consistently strong. Fibrec is good on cotton and wool, fair on silk. Colorfastness is good, and no special fixing procedure is required. Fibrec is relatively simple to use, salt and washing soda acting as assistants in the dyeing process. There may be some difficulty dissolving the dye thoroughly; it has a tendency to clump.

Craftool

Craftool manufactures direct dyes for cotton and acid dyes for silk. We tested only the direct dyes for cotton which require the use of salt as an assistant. This dye comes in a paper envelope containing 1 ounce of dyestuff and sells for $1.00 a package. As far as we know, it is not available in retail art-supply stores but must be ordered from the catalog of the Craftool Company. The packages open easily, but then the dye must be stored in jars or other containers.

Craftool dyes are easy to use and to mix. The dyeing process takes from 20 minutes to an hour, depending upon the depth of color desired. Salt is added at the beginning of the dyeing process.

The colors tested tended to be somewhat muddy and were far from being true shades of red, yellow, and blue. But while the color was not clear, it was strong; and all three colors dyed with equal intensity. Of all the dyes tested, Craftool gave the most unusual shades of blue, yellow, and red. These dyes are only fair in terms of colorfastness; they will lose color when washed, and dry-cleaning or careful hand washing is recommended. Ironing the fabric after it is dyed is suggested to help fix the dye.

Cushing

Cushing dyes come in many colors and can be used on all natural fibers. They are packaged in aluminum-foil envelopes containing approximately ½ ounce, and, as far as we know, they can be obtained only from the manufacturer. Cushing dyes sell for twenty-five cents a package, by far the cheapest batik dye on the market.

These dyes are simple to use and do not seem to present any problems in mixing. Dyeing time varies from 20 minutes to an hour, depending upon the intensity of color desired. Although salt is the recommended assistant in the instructions, we suggest substituting acetic acid when dyeing wool or silk.

Cushing dyes produced clear color with good intensity on cotton, silk, and wool. While the color was strong, the three colors tested were not true shades of blue, red, and yellow—the blue was a strong aqua, for example. They dyed with equal intensity on cotton and wool; on silk, however, the red appeared to be apricot, while on cotton it was more of a red-orange. The blue and the yellow maintained the same color tone on all the fabrics dyed.

The colorfastness of Cushing dyes is only fair, and dry-cleaning or hand washing is strongly recommended. Ironing will help fix the dye.

Sennelier

This French dye, available at a few retail art-supply stores in this country, comes in small metal tubes containing about an ounce of dyestuff. Each tube sells for $1.25, making Sennelier the most expensive dye for batik reviewed here.

These dyes are simple to use, requiring no assistant as far as we know. The dyeing time is relatively short— usually no longer than 5 or 10 minutes—since the dyes are absorbed quickly. Although the dye can be stored easily in its original package, it does have a sensitivity to moisture and must be stored in a dry place; otherwise the dye may solidify in the tubes, making it difficult to extract.

Sennelier dyes gave excellent color intensity on silk and good color results on cotton and silk. All three colors took with equal intensity on silk and wool; on cotton, however, the color results were variable, the red tending to wash out.

These dyes are only fair in terms of colorfastness and seem to be highly sensitive to light. There are no known fixing procedures required.

To summarize our evaluation of batik dyes and to consolidate all the information for easy reference, we contrived a simple chart. You may find it useful when using and experimenting with dyes. In addition we have included a list of dyes and dye manufacturers, with their addresses, and also the names and addresses of a few retail art-supply stores where dyes can be obtained, in the List of Suppliers, page 151.

A BRIEF REVIEW OF BATIK DYES

Dye Brand	Type of Dye	Fiber	Assistant	Price	Availability
Craftool	Direct	Cotton	Salt	$1.00 per ounce	Mail order from manufacturer
Cushing	Direct/acid	All natural fibers	Salt or acetic acid	$ .25 per ½ ounce	Mail order from manufacturer
Dylon	Fiber-reactive	All natural fibers	Salt and washing soda	$ .50 per ½ ounce	Art-supply stores
Fibrec	Fiber-reactive	All natural fibers	Salt and washing soda	$1.00 per ½ ounce	Art-supply stores
Pylam	Fiber-reactive	All natural fibers	Salt and washing soda	$1.00 per ounce	Mail order from manufacturer
Sennelier	Unknown	All natural fibers	None	$1.25 per ounce	Art-supply stores

Packaging	Dyeing Process	Color	Color Fastness	Fixing Dye
Paper envelope	Simple: 20–60 minutes	Somewhat muddy; all colors consistently intense	Fair	Ironing
Foil envelope	Simple: 20–60 minutes	Good, clear in all colors. Not consistent on silk	Fair	Ironing
Small round tins; difficult to open	Simple: 30 minutes; requires stirring; difficult to dissolve	Good on wool and cotton, fair on silk. Certain colors not consistent	Good	Not required
Plastic packets	Simple: 30 minutes; some difficulty dissolving	Good on wool and cotton, fair on silk. All colors consistently good.	Good	Not required
Jars (good for storage)	Simple: 30 minutes; requires stirring	Best on cotton; good on wool and silk. All colors consistently good.	Good	Not required
Tubes	Simple: less than 30 minutes	Best of all dyes in intensity. All colors consistently good.	Fair	Not required

PART II
THE BATIK PROCESS

Design

Here you are. You are standing in front of a clean table, frame and thumbtacks ready, newspaper down, and you turn your wax on. You take a piece of cloth—newly purchased—from a bag, a beautiful, softly shining piece of silk, and begin tacking it to the frame. Stretched taut on the frame, the fabric stares at you, an empty, white, undefined space, a virgin field, waiting for form and definition, waiting for you to give it life.

This is the way it begins in batik. You start with "nothing." You create or make "something." Through batik you transform a lifeless void into an expression—through line, shape, color, and texture—of yourself. When you begin you have before you an open country with no boundaries, with endless possibilities to go in infinite directions. Where will you go? What roads will you take? What turns and detours? And what is your destination?

With batik—as with all things we do—there are three stages in the experience. There is the beginning and the end, and, in between those two points, the process of *doing* itself. The beginning and the end are perhaps the most exhilarating stages. The beginning is filled with excitement and anticipation of what will potentially be, perhaps also laced with a little trepidation, or with a hesitation to explore and define limits. The end gives a sense of accomplishment, of mastery, of power and control, of completion, of pleasure or disappointment. The end is also a time of renewal, of seeing one's own development, growth, skill, and needs, of meeting oneself again in a new form of expression and trying to learn from it.

In between those two dramatic points is the middle stage—the dynamic process of creation. This process is like a journey between two points; its essential nature is movement and change. It is the "doing" part, making decisions and taking action, with each decision and consequent action limiting and defining the next possible decision and action. This is the process through which the formless takes form, where the empty cloth receives definition through the development of a design, where the lifeless becomes a statement of life.

Transforming that new piece of fabric, stretched on a frame but without shape or form, into an original hand-rendered design on cloth, using wax and dye—this is the process of design in batik. It is this process that we wish to discuss and describe in this section of our book. But as much as we wish to convey to you the experience of realizing a design through batik, we also find it extremely difficult to do so. There are at least two reasons for this difficulty.

First, and quite obviously, developing a design is not an intellectual process (although the mind is involved), and it is not something we think about or articulate to ourselves. It is something that we just do, or that happens. It comes more from an emotional place inside, and seems to come through almost organically. For this reason it is not something easily talked about or even known. In many ways it is undefinable as an experience, although certain principles, assumptions, or considerations in the pursuit of a design can, and will be, articulated.

Second, not only is it difficult to describe or communicate our experience of making a design, but it is almost impossible for you to learn how to do it from a book. The process of designing is really a personal experience *which you learn through doing*, through trying to express something of yourself in a particular medium and discovering in that process your own concept of design.

There are no rules in design. We cannot tell you what to do, whether you should put a line here or there, or what color you should use, or how to create a feeling of movement which *you* wish to communicate. Color, form, line, movement—these are all elements of design which you will fit together to make a whole that is right for you.

What we can do is to offer some guidelines for designing specifically in the medium of batik. Each craft, each medium, because of the nature of its materials or its potential function, has its own characteristics which affect how you approach design in that medium. For example, in ceramics you make three-dimensional objects, and therefore a foremost consideration in ceramic design is form. In leather or wood, you usually do not work with color as a major element in design, but rather you use the natural color and feeling of the material itself to enhance the design.

CONCEIVING A DESIGN

In batik you work on a flat, one-dimensional surface, rather like a painting. Form is created through composition and the illusion of depth and space. In batik, color is a major and essential element of design; it is through multiple dyeing and waxing that a design is developed, that form is defined and differentiated, that a blank white surface is transformed into a hand-designed fabric.

While design in batik presents problems similar to those presented in painting, there is one very distinctive and, for the batik craftsman, critical difference between painting and design in batik. Unlike painting, in which you apply color to canvas or paper, in batik you are always applying wax to *prevent* color from appearing on the cloth. When you paint wax onto the fabric in batik, you are not painting color on or adding color to the cloth, but rather you are protecting areas of the cloth from obtaining color. The wax acts as a shield against the addition of color; it masks those colors that already exist rather than introducing new color. It is the areas that are *unwaxed* that are exposed to new color.

This fact inherent in the batik medium requires a particular conceptual approach to design in batik, a mental attitude which you must develop as you define your design with wax. What you are really doing when you cover areas with wax is making a negative, as in photography. When you look at a photographic negative, areas that are dark are those areas that will be light when the photograph is developed. When you have finished your first waxing and you look at the fabric before it is dyed, the areas that are covered with wax (and appear darker) are those areas that will be white (or your lightest color); whereas all the other areas that are unwaxed and white (or your lightest color) will become darker as they are exposed to dye.

This is a difficult concept to communicate in words, but something easily understood in the doing. We have had some very amusing—or not so amusing—experiences in trying to communicate this conceptual attitude to students. Often, in the middle of doing their first batik, students will realize that the design they are creating is the reverse of what they had intended; the areas they thought would be blue were going to be white and the white areas would be blue. Of course, the end result is not always disappointing; in fact, sometimes the result is much more exciting and satisfying than the intended design. Certainly, it is more surprising!

However, in learning a craft one finds satisfaction in an ability to attain certain results, in mastering and controlling the technique in order to create what one wishes. In this respect the concept of creating a negative with the wax must consistently guide you in the realization of your design. And this concept will become more familiar to you (and eventually, second nature, so that you automatically approach your work with it in mind) the more you do batik, the more you experience the techniques of design in batik.

THE ELEMENT OF COLOR

Another conceptual element of design in batik is that the design is *built up* through color. Each color is a *separate* step in the development of a design. Instead of working on one area of your fabric, for example, and filling in all the different colors in that area as you might do in painting, in batik you work on the cloth *as a whole*. Furthermore, each color in your design essentially involves a separate step in creating the design: you introduce each color, from lightest to darkest, one at a time, blocking out with wax all areas you wish to remain the color they are, and then dyeing the cloth.

When you approach design in batik, you see it as a whole and differentiate (at least in your mind) the different areas of color that will compose the design. Then you start to build up the design, color by color. First, you cover all those areas in the design that are to be white, and dye them. Then you cover the first color with wax, wherever you wish it to appear in your design, and dye it. Then you cover the next color with wax and dye the fabric, and so on . . . until all colors have been added and the design is completed. Each time you add a color to your design by covering it with wax, be sure you block out all the areas you wish to remain that color, because once it is dyed a new color, there is no going back.

In general, when you approach your batik, you visualize the total result you wish to realize and, *at the same time*, you break down and differentiate the various color elements of your design, adding each color element one at a time while maintaining a vision of the whole.

Another aspect of design particular to batik, and one that also must be kept in mind as you carry out your design, is that through the process of adding color upon color, one at a time, the new color obtained in the dyeing process is always the result of a *combination* of two colors: the color of the cloth before it is submerged in the dye and the color of the dyebath itself. The aspect of using color in designing batik will be discussed in greater depth in Color, page 96.

FUNCTION AND DESIGN

Beyond the basic principles of conceptualization in batik design, more practical determinants must be considered which also act as guidelines in your approach to design in batik. The foremost is the *function* of the fabric you are designing. In all crafts there is an interrelationship between design and function. For instance, when a potter designs a teapot, its shape, volume, and line will be determined by its function—the spout will be placed in such a way so that the pot will contain a good amount of liquid without dribbling, and the handle will be large enough and placed in such a manner that the user will

OPPOSITE: *Building a design waxing-by-waxing, color-by-color and shape-by-shape.*

not burn himself. The design of the pot is delineated in part by its function—to hold and serve tea. In a similar way, when designing a purse a leather craftsman must consider how it will be carried (by hand or on the shoulder?), how much it will hold, what a functional closure is, and how all of these practical aspects can be integrated into a design that has integrity in his eyes. A candlemaker must design candles that not only are pleasing to the eye but also burn evenly and effectively.

In batik, function also interacts with design. A batik is essentially a piece of cloth which is hand-designed. Its function is connected first of all to the fact that it is fabric, and therefore its functional possibilities include all the potential uses fabric can be put to—dresses, pillows, curtains, ties, scarves, shawls, wall hangings, bedspreads, tablecloths, shirts. Whatever its function, the design you pursue in creating your batik must harmonize with the use to which it will be put. The harmony between design and function is always a guideline for the craftsman.

In batik, for example, you may be making fabric for a man's tie. In this case you would make a small or intricate pattern, perhaps use more somber or solid colors. Or you may be designing fabric for pillows, and your design approach in this case would include a consideration of the environment in which the pillows will be placed— the color, the feeling tone, the architectural style, the dynamics or function of the room itself. You may decide to pick up and pursue in your pillow fabric a motif already existing in the environment, or you might want to introduce a contrasting, dramatic complement to what already exists. And this is all a part of the interaction between design and function. Perhaps you are designing fabric for a wall hanging; again, the function influences the design. In this case you will consider the space in which it will hang, the dimensions, the lighting, the colors and feeling surrounding it, the distance from which it will be viewed. The design of the wall hanging must be able to carry visually, because its very purpose is to add visual interest to an environment.

MATERIALS AND DESIGN

Besides function, the materials with which you work also influence and affect the design direction you pursue. In batik you work with cloth, which comes in a wide variety of textures, weights, weaves, and sheens, and these qualities must be considered when approaching design. Whatever the design feeling will be, it must complement the feeling of the fabric itself.

Often certain aspects of the fabric will limit the design possibilities. For example, heavyweight or thickly-woven fabrics such as heavy wool, muslin, or raw silk will not permit fine-lined or finely detailed designs; the wax simply will not adhere sufficiently to obtain enough clarity for an intricate design. Therefore, if you were to work with these fibers, you would use bolder designs, worked with large brushes. Texture will also influence design. With any highly textured fabric such as silk linen, burlap or some raw silks, it is impossible to create fine lines or to work effectively with the *tjanting*. Somehow you must integrate your design with the texture of the fabric in order to enhance the qualities of both.

Alternately, you can choose fabric which will work for a particular design you may already have in mind, selecting that fabric that most effectively conveys your design idea. But in either case—whether selecting fabric for a specific design or designing for a specific fabric—the relationship of design and material must be remembered and utilized.

THE TIME ELEMENT

Another practical determinant of design is the amount of time you wish to spend in creating your batik. If you are limited in time, you will want to make a simple design using only a few colors so that there will be fewer steps in the waxing and dyeing process. If your time is un-limited, then your design can be more intricate and you need not feel compelled to limit the number of colors.

METHODS FOR APPROACHING DESIGN IN BATIK

With the major conceptual and practical aspects of de-sign in batik in mind, you might like to consider two different ways of approaching batik design. These are not intended to be explicit instructions in design but rather two contrasting methods of advancing toward an as-yet-unrealized design.

One approach in designing your batik is to begin with a specific drawing. First you work up several design possibilities on paper, outlining the various forms and shapes, even indicating the colors to be used. Then, select one of your sketched designs that you feel would be most effectively rendered in the batik medium. Your drawings can be based on experiences you have had, on things you have seen in nature such as trees or flowers, symbols that are important to you, or traditional design motifs found in design books such as Navaho Indian rug designs, traditional hex signs, or geometric mosaic patterns. Once your design is clearly worked up, begin to transfer the design to the cloth, either by sketching it first in soft pencil or charcoal onto the cloth or by sketching directly with wax. In transferring the drawing to the cloth it is important to be clear about which areas will become which colors; it may be helpful to indicate this either on the drawing or on the cloth itself. Each waxing and dyeing fills in new areas of your outlined design until the design is completed.

A second approach to design in batik is to work toward

your design spontaneously. Instead of developing your design on paper first, develop your design directly on the cloth. When working in this way it is good to know in advance what you will use the cloth for, because that will give direction to your design. Also it is helpful to have something in mind as you begin—an image or feeling you wish to create, an object or symbol you wish to render, a texture or pattern of movement you wish to suggest. Then start painting with the wax or working with the *tjanting*, remembering that the wax is covering your first color, probably white, and that this is the first step of a total design.

This freehand approach to design allows for experimentation and discovery. You might explore the different textural effects created with the various batik tools, or even experiment with other objects and materials that you could use to apply wax, like crumpled paper, sponges, or toothbrushes. You might explore different design motifs by repeating them, in slightly varying ways, with each waxing. You might take some basic shape, such as a triangle, and overlap triangle over triangle with each particular color that you dye the cloth, thus building up a design of one simple form. You might experiment with the *tjanting* by making continuous lines, running in varying directions, creating a second design using something simple—just a line.

The point in this exploration, and in exploring batik in general, is to be open to the endless possibilities which truly exist. It is a time to work more freely, more loosely, without worrying about "making a mistake" and without worrying about the result. It is a time of learning. A reminder in working this way: it is important *not* to wax every area, especially if you wish to dye and rewax the cloth several times. As you are working, allow space for additional color and design. Relax. Take your time and be simple when you start.

Color

It is impossible to talk about design in batik without a consideration of color, because color and design in this medium are inseparable. Essentially there are two possible means of creating design on fabric with color. One way is to introduce shape and form to an already woven, solid piece of cloth by painting or submerging parts of cloth into dye. This is what is done in batik, as well as other dyeing methods such as tie-dye and silk-screening. Another way is introduce colored fibers themselves into the design such as through weaving or embroidering. In either case, the design is created through color, through defining different-colored areas either with dye or with colored threads.

Not only does color define design in batik, but color gives life to the design. It is dynamic; it is vibrant,

PLATE 13: *Wall Hanging—"Terrain" by Laura Adasko. Batik on silk shantung. Loaned by Takayo Doran, New York.*

96

expressive, it is active and reactive, it is emotional, it is moody. It can be dramatic, or powerful, or subtle, or subdued. Of course, the feeling or atmosphere that color communicates depends entirely on how it is used; color is not absolute, it is relative. It is really the play of color against color, color accented by color, or the combination of different colors or color tones that creates the design effect. It is by learning and mastering the effects of color that you will begin to be able to communicate the feeling or atmosphere you wish to embody in your designs.

In working with color, you must first decide the overall impression or mood you wish your batik design to have. Then consider what colors or combination of colors will convey that impression for you. The choice of color in relation to mood is, of course, subjective; one person's blue may be another person's red.

THE DIMENSIONS OF COLOR

Warm and Cool Colors

Color has many dimensions. Becoming familiar with these dimensions and utilizing them will give you greater control in your batik work. Among them is, first, the dimension of temperature. Some colors are inherently warm: red and yellow or combinations thereof. Certain colors are, by nature, cool: blue and green are primary examples. There are also colors that, in certain contexts or in certain shades or hues, can be *either* warm or cool— brown or purple, for example. The dimension of warmth or coolness is not simply inherent in the color itself, but is dependent upon the juxtaposition of color and upon the shade or intensity of the colors used. For example,

PLATE 14: *Velveteen Pillows. Batik by Laura Adasko. Appliquéd by Tamala Design, New York.*

97

when certain shades of blue and green are used together in a design, the green will have warmth in comparison with the surrounding blue. However, that same shade of green when used in a design with yellow will appear much cooler. In one design a purple will appear cool next to a warm red, but in another design it will seem warm juxtaposed to black. Obviously, the dimension of temperature in color is relative, dependent upon the context in which the color appears. A major concern in batik design is to establish the color context of your design. Is your design, in general, warm or cool? Then, within that context, establish a balance between cold and warm elements, in order to convey the intended impression, yet add contrast.

Light and Dark Colors
Another dimension of color is lightness and darkness. If your overall design impression is light, you will use either light colors such as yellow, pink, beige, or light hues of various colors such as pale blue, light green, or coral. In creating a darker mood you would choose darker colors such as purple, brown, or black, or darker and more intense shades of colors such as wine, navy blue, or olive green.

Luminosity
Related to lightness or darkness is the luminosity of color. Certain colors or shades of colors have a quality of luminosity, which creates a certain illusion of depth and aliveness. Some shades of yellow, blue, green, or orange will convey this effect, if it is desired.

Transparency and Opaqueness
Luminosity is connected with another dimension of color, the dimension of transparency and opaqueness. Every color or shade of color is either transparent or opaque,

and this quality of color should be exploited in the pursuit of a design. A luminous, transparent blue, for example, will give an illusion of depth, as if light is coming from below. One might choose to use such a shade of blue in a design intended to convey the feeling of water. Transparency or opaqueness is also connected to the illusion of depth in a design; opaque colors create a much flatter surface, whereas transparent colors give a feeling of depth or distance. Often it is the combination of opaque and transparent colors that gives richness to a design, with certain areas appearing flat and more solid, other areas appearing deeper, with shifting movement. The juxtaposition of opaque and transparent colors will give a dynamic quality to a design and will create a certain kind of energy or movement.

Movement

Another dimension of color with which you will become familiar as you work is that of movement. Certain colors in certain contexts will appear to advance and others to recede; in other contexts, the advancing colors may recede and the receding colors will advance. The important thing to keep in mind is that color *moves*. The *way* it moves depends upon the shade and intensity of the color and the combination and placement of colors within the design. For example, pink and orange are very active, aggressive colors which will generally come forward in a design, and when used together will play against each other to create tension and movement. Turquoise and lime green are advancing colors, and when used together in a design will generate movement and energy. Plum next to yellow or orange-golds will recede; yet when placed next to a forest green, plum will advance. Certain colors are primarily active—yellow, bright pink, orange, fuchsia, turquoise—whereas certain other colors will generally recede—black, brown, blue, darker reds and purples. But we again stress that it is the context of the colors that creates the movement.

Harmony and Dissonance

Another dimension to consider is that of harmony, and the corollary to harmony, dissonance. Certain color combinations are harmonious; other combinations are dissonant. Harmonious colors tend to create an effect of calmness, of subtlety and quietness. Dissonant colors imply activity, chaos, loudness, disunity. Soft blues and purples are harmonious; orange and green together are dissonant. Lavender and green will harmonize; violet and yellow will not. Generally, colors that harmonize with each other are close in tone but vary in intensity, whereas colors that are dissonant are close in intensity but vary in tone. Again, harmony or disharmony lies in the context in which the colors are used.

Strength and Weakness

Another way to look at color is in terms of strength or weakness. Certain colors in certain contexts will appear weak, others strong. Of course the strength or weakness of a color is interrelated with the other dimensions discussed, but in considering color in relation to design it is helpful to consider which parts of the design you wish to emphasize or make predominant and then choose colors that will convey that emphasis.

LIMITATIONS IN THE COLOR-OVER-COLOR TECHNIQUE

These general considerations of color in relation to design can act as guidelines in your efforts to realize certain color effects, but their application is limited by certain very specific characteristics of the batik process itself. A familiarity with these limitations is crucial if you wish to develop control of the batik medium.

In batik you usually dye color over color (except if you remove wax in between dyes, which will be discussed later). Because of the nature of the color-over-color technique, you must always work from the lightest to the darkest color. Obviously, if you dyed your cloth dark brown first, you could not achieve a yellow at a later point in the dyeing and waxing process.

Second, because of the process inherent in batik of dyeing color over color, the resultant color is always a *combination* of two colors: the color of the cloth just before it is submerged in a new dyebath and the color of the dyebath itself. In a sense this can act as a limitation in terms of the possibility of achieving certain colors in a design, since the resultant color is always a synthesis of two colors. For example, if you were to place a yellow fabric in a blue dye, you would not achieve blue, but a combination of blue and yellow—i.e., green. There are basic color combinations with which you will become familiar as you work in this medium. They are:

> Red and blue—purple
> Yellow and blue—green
> Yellow and red—orange
> Green and red—brown
> Green and orange—brown
> Purple and red—wine
> Blue and green—peacock or turquoise blue
> Blue and black—navy blue
> Pink and yellow—peach or coral
> Pink and purple—fuchsia
> Yellow and green—lime
> Green and red and purple and blue—black
> (hopefully)

There are many other possible color combinations, but they are more dependent on the intensity of the two colors involved. In fact, learning about the effect of com-

Batik dyes.

bining colors of different intensity will help you over-come the limitations presented in dyeing color over color. In fact, we see these limitations as a challenge, as something that forces us to explore, experiment, and play with color so that our work becomes full of discovery and surprise. Through this exploration we have discovered color combinations that we would never have expected, and perhaps will never achieve again!

A general rule in regard to intensity of color is that, if you dye an intense color over a weak color, the result will be more in the direction of the intense color. For example, if you were to dye a royal blue over a very pale yellow, you might get a blue, not a green. Another color we have discovered is the result of combining green and purple: when we dye a strong green over a relatively strong purple we are able to get a forest green; when we dye a strong purple over a mild green, we have achieved a plum or wine-purple. When dyeing a strong yellow over a moderately strong fuchsia, it is possible to get a gold-yellow or rust.

Another possibility is to dye a color weak in intensity over a stronger color: a weak red over a strong yellow will give an orange-gold; a pale blue over a strong yellow will give you a lime green or chartreuse. The principle is that when you are combining a strong color with a weak color—*no matter which comes first*—the resulting color will always go in the direction of the more intense color. And if the colors are equal in intensity, whether both are weak or both are strong, then the resulting color will be an equal blend of the two. For example, wine is the result of a red and purple of equal intensity, or orange results from a combination of yellow and red of about the same intensity. A pale lavender is achieved by dyeing a weak blue over a pale pink. If you wish to create a batik in more muted color tones, work with weaker shades and their combinations, perhaps even adding a touch of black or navy blue to the dye to achieve a muted feeling.

Sometimes when dyeing a strong color over a strong color you end up with a muddy shade. Although this muddiness is difficult to remedy, it might be possible to clarify the color effect by dyeing your batik in a very strong dyebath, if only to create a contrast. Another possibility is to dye the batik black the next time—if it is not black at this point already!

We feel that in doing batik there is no such thing as a mistake. If you end up with a color you did not intend, work with it, play with your dyes, be adventurous, find out what colors are possible, see how you can integrate your new color into your design. In this way you will learn more about using dyes and achieving color.

OTHER DYEING METHODS IN BATIK

So far we have talked about the basic and most common method of using dyes and achieving color in batik—the method of dipping cloth into dyebaths, one after the other, the process of achieving a third color by dyeing color over color. There are other possible ways to realize certain color effects in the batik medium that do not involve dyeing over color. These methods can be used when you wish to achieve certain color combinations that you could not achieve by dyeing color over color. For example, if you want a true blue and a true red in your design, you would not use the overdye technique but rather would choose one of the methods described below to realize this combination.

The Wax-Removal Method

One alternate method of achieving color involves the removal of wax between steps in the dyeing and waxing process. In this approach you wax and dye the batik, then iron out the wax, thus removing the resist, and start waxing anew. Since you will use this method when you want colors that cannot be achieved by dyeing color over color, you will want most areas of your cloth to remain white, at least initially, because it is only the white areas that will become pure colors and not a combination of colors.

Hence your first waxing, when the cloth is white, will be extensive, as you will cover with wax not only those areas you wish to remain white, but also all those areas that, when the wax is removed from them and they are exposed to fresh dye, will become uncombined, true colors. For example, if your design requires both a true red and a true blue, your first waxing will involve covering all the areas you wish to be blue as well as all the areas you wish to be white; then you dye the cloth red. Next, after the cloth has dried, you will remove *all* the wax and then wax the fabric a second time, this time covering the areas you wish to be white and those areas you wish to be red, leaving exposed to the dye those areas intended to be blue. And now you submerge the cloth in a blue dyebath. In this way you will achieve a design made up of white, blue, and red, and even purple on areas that are a combination of red and blue dyes.

There are a few possible disadvantages to using this method which you should keep in mind. One disadvantage is that it takes quite a bit more time than leaving the wax on and building up your design by dyeing color over color. Another, perhaps more critical disadvantage is that it is difficult to remove the wax entirely from the fabric in such a way that it will not interfere with the design, unless you are working on a small piece of fabric. Ironing out the wax, and even using benzene, will leave a residue of wax or oil from the wax which can continue to act as a resist and spoil your design.

Painting Dye Onto Fabric

Another possibility for applying color to your batik is to paint the dye onto the cloth rather than to submerge the cloth in dye. In this way you are not dyeing color over color, but applying different colors to different areas of a white fabric, creating a multicolored design by this process. Of course, all possible colors can be put together in this way, because you are not limited to the mixed color combinations that result from dyeing color over color.

To use this dyeing technique, outline all the different color areas with wax, using a small brush to create a thin line. The wax outline must fully penetrate the cloth. Next, with a sponge, wet the cloth in those areas where you intend to paint; this will help the cloth absorb the dye. Then paint a concentrate of dye, either with a brush or a piece of surgical cotton, in the area within the waxed outline. The waxed outline prevents the color from spreading out beyond its boundaries. Each outlined area can become a different color, and it is even possible to achieve gradations of color within a waxbound area. The resultant effect of this process of applying color is very different from that of the true batik method. Because of the outlines around each color area, there is a preciseness and a clarity of design, and, at the same time, a lack of the dynamism that is created when colors play against each other without being separated by a white line. Furthermore, with this technique there is no crackle, the signature of batik.

This method requires a knowledge of dyes suitable for painting, of the special methods necessary for preparing them as a concentrate, and of the appropriate procedures for fixing the dyes. In working on silk you must use acid dye and also must steam the cloth after finishing your piece in order to fix the dye. (See our chapter Dyes, page 53.)

After completing your design by painting with dyes, you may want to cover the entire design area with wax and dye the entire cloth by submersion in a darker or contrasting dyebath, which adds the distinctive crackle of batik to your design and also creates a background color.

Although these two ways—painting with dyes and removing wax between dyes—offer other possibilities of achieving color in your design, we much prefer the method really inherent to the batik process, the method of dyeing color over color, giving to batik its own special coloration and also its own unique problems. We have often run across a disappointed face when a student has realized there are certain color limitations in the dipping and dyeing method, but the more you work in this medium, the more you see the possibilities that exist within the limitations. In a sense it is the limitations of color in the traditional batik method of overdyeing which call forth the creativity, imagination, and exploration that allow you to grow with the craft.

Technique

In this chapter we want to talk about the use of tools and wax in relation to the development of design in batik. Just as the use of dyes and the process of dyeing color over color present both certain limitations and certain possibilities to the batik craftsman, the special characteristics of wax and the tools both circumscribe and expand the design possibilities in batik.

USING THE *TJANTING*

The tools that you will consistently use in batik require familiarity and experience in application before you can develop mastery in this medium. The *tjanting* particularly requires a great deal of control which you will learn only by using it. As a tool the *tjanting* offers the possibility of creating fine lines, or intricate designs and textured ef-

OPPOSITE: *Some batik tools: brushes,* tjantings, *wax and fabric.*

108

fects; therefore you will probably want to become adept in its use.

In using the *tjanting*, it is essential to develop a certain rhythm in moving this tool from the wax pot to the cloth. If you move too slowly, the wax will cool too much and will not flow onto or penetrate the cloth sufficiently to act as a resist. If you move too quickly, you may splatter the wax from the cup, and also you will have less control. As you work, you will find the right movement from wax pot to cloth, a movement that will soon become automatic and second nature to you.

While you are moving the *tjanting* to the cloth, it is helpful, we have found, to keep a piece of cloth or paper towel under the spout of the *tjanting* so that wax will not drip from the spout *until* it is placed on the cloth where you will begin to develop your design. This preserves the maximum amount of hot wax in the *tjanting* cup; more importantly, it prevents wax from dripping either onto your table or floor or onto parts of your fabric where it is not desired. As you move from one area of your fabric to another while working with the *tjanting*, you will want to cover the spout whenever you move across those areas on which you do not want wax to appear. In short, placing paper under the spout gives you control in applying the wax *only* where you want it to go.

Once you have placed the *tjanting* on the cloth and are ready to begin working with it, remove the paper from the spout and start waxing, moving the *tjanting* quickly and smoothly. As you will see, the wax will flow rapidly from the spout, and if you want fine lines you must move quickly. The flow of the wax will depend on the angle

TOP RIGHT: *Filling the* tjanting *with liquid wax.*

BOTTOM: *Keep a piece of fabric or paper towel under the* tjanting *to prevent spills.*

110

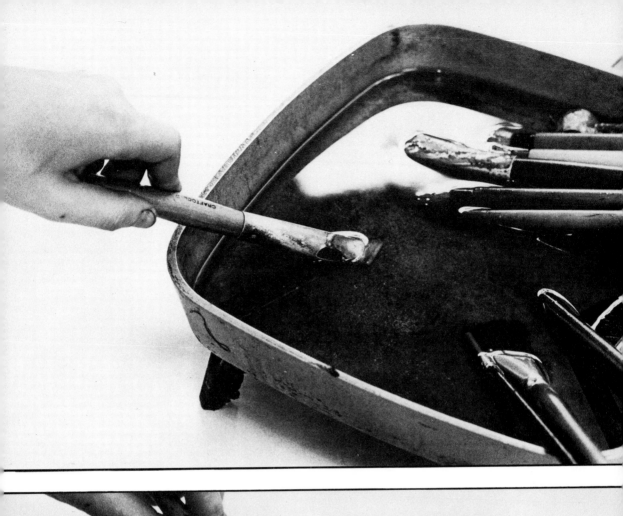
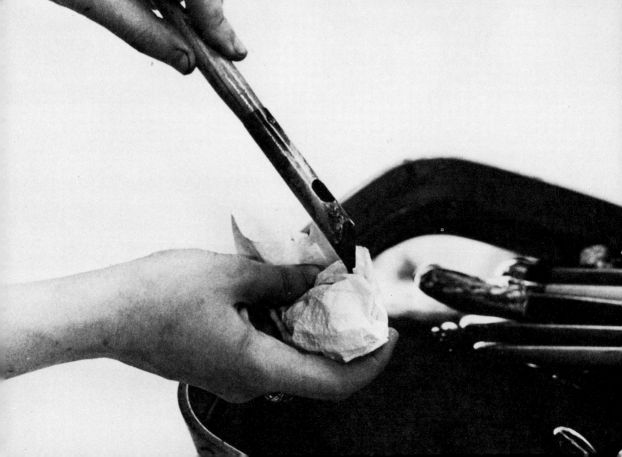

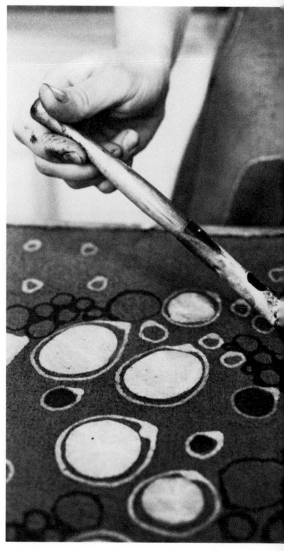

LEFT: *Move the* tjanting *quickly and smoothly across the cloth.*

RIGHT: *Apply even, firm pressure when using the* tjanting.

PLATE 15: *Wall Hanging—"In Space" by
Laura Adasko. Batik on silk shantung.
Loaned by Crates, a gallery in Miami,
Florida.*

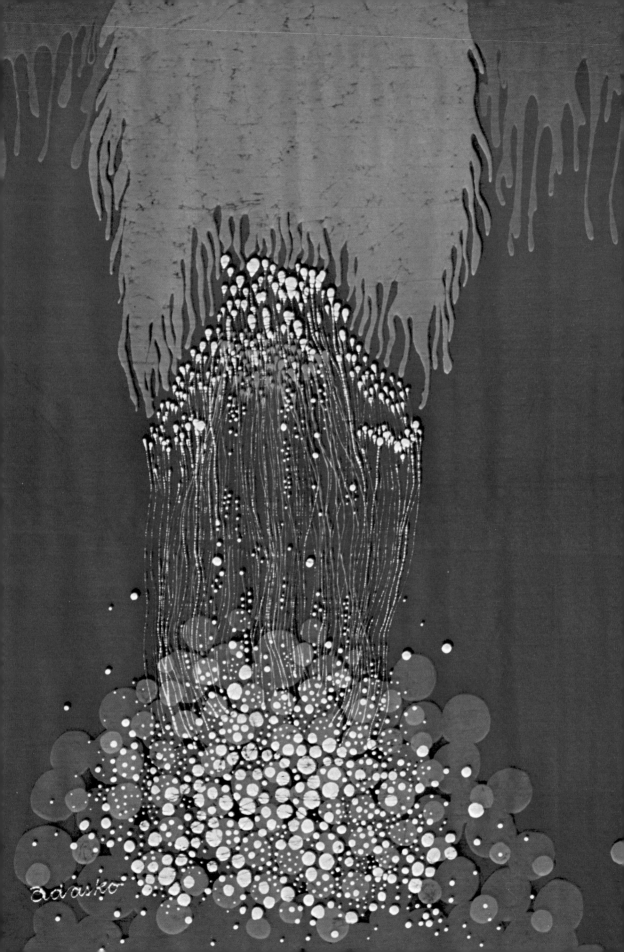

at which you hold the spout; as you work and use up the wax in the cup, you will tip the spout at a more severe angle to facilitate the flow of wax. Eventually, you will learn how far you can go with one bowlful of wax and how often you will have to refill your *tjanting;* it might be useful to consider this when working on your design, that is, to figure out at what points you will be able to stop and at what points you will want to have a full *tjanting.*

Another technical aspect of using the *tjanting* is the proper amount of pressure applied to the *tjanting* point where it touches the fabric. If there is too much pressure, the *tjanting* will not move or will move in a jerky fashion, and the wax will accumulate and form splotches. If there is too little pressure, the wax will flow too rapidly from the spout, thus forming thick rather than thin lines. What is required is to find the proper amount of pressure for the type of line you wish to create and the particular *tjanting* you are using. Again, this is something you will learn in working with the tool.

USING BRUSHES

Although learning to work with the *tjanting* will take more time and skill than learning to work with brushes, there are still some technical aspects of brushwork that are important to consider. In working with a brush as well as with the *tjanting,* you will want to work rapidly so that the wax will remain hot long enough to penetrate the cloth when it is applied. Moving in a rapid manner requires that you be careful not to dribble wax from the brush in places where you do not want it. Again, we

PLATE 16: *Wall Hanging—"Golden Circles" by Laura Adasko. Batik on silk satin. Loaned by Global Village, New York.*

113

suggest that you hold a piece of cloth or paper towel under the brush as you move across your fabric. Furthermore, it is important to use brushes large enough or thick enough to hold a good quantity of wax and maintain its temperature so that you will be able to work on a sufficient portion of your design before you must refill the brush with wax.

It is also important to select the proper-sized brush for the area of the design you are waxing; if you are filling in a large area with wax, you will work with a large brush, perhaps a household paintbrush, and if you are making smaller shapes or lines, you will work with a small bamboo brush, the kind used in Oriental brush painting. We strongly recommend Oriental brushes, because they are especially well-suited to retaining the wax in the brush so that it will flow smoothly for a long time. With brushes, as well as with the *tjanting*, you will learn a certain rhythm or flow of movement as you apply the wax to your designs, a certain rapidity and smoothness in the movement as well as control. This rhythm becomes a part of the way you work, automatic and natural.

The kind or size of brush you choose to use, as well as the type of stroke you make in using it, can determine the textured effect you will achieve. Essentially, texture, or variation in texture, is created in batik by the degree of solidity of wax applied in different areas. An area completely and evenly covered with wax will appear non-textured, except for the crackle that appears there. An area that is not solidly covered with wax, where the wax has not penetrated evenly or fully, will appear textured.

There are two ways in which you can achieve a textured effect by using brushes. One way is to use a brush that has very little hot wax on it. In painting with the brush, you will create a rough, multilined, woven-looking surface, appearing almost like interlacing, even plaid-like, fibers or threads. This is called the dry-brush technique, for the very reason that the brush you use

A household paintbrush is useful for filling in large areas.

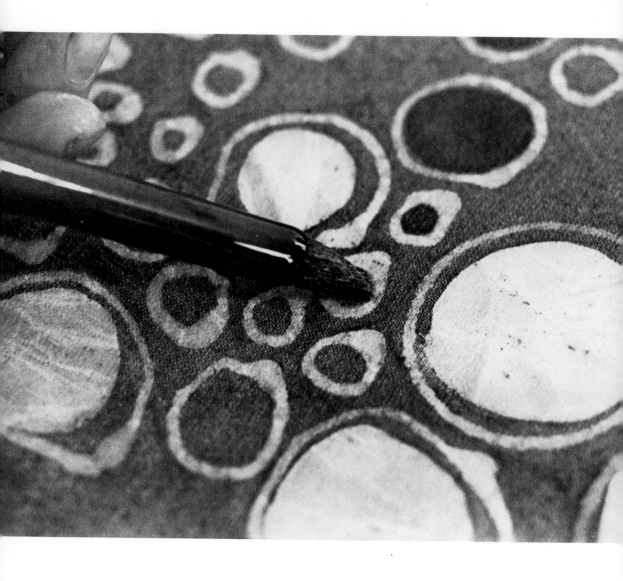

Oriental paintbrushes are best for filling in small areas.

is essentially dry. That is, it contains very little hot wax, so the wax does not enter the cloth as a liquid but rather imprints the quality of the brush (fine hair) onto the cloth.

A second method of achieving texture with a brush is to use varying strokes. By applying the brush quickly, moving it onto and off the fabric almost simultaneously, by changing the angles of the brush as you move it across the fabric, or by varying the amount of pressure on the brush as you work with it—all of these techniques will create texture. For example, if you are working with a large household brush, by applying the wax first with the broad width of the brush and then turning the brush and applying the wax with its thin side, you will create a contrast in texture by utilizing two dimensions of the brush. Or by changing the pressure on your brush in some areas from heavy to light, you will achieve an intermingling of solidity and featheriness.

CONTROLLING CRACKLE

Beyond the use of tools to create texture, the crackle of wax inherent in the batik process creates its own special texture, one which the batik craftsman learns to use in the creation of a design. Whether crackle is used or avoided depends on the design effect desired, and the amount of crackle achieved is, in part, determined by the proportions of beeswax and paraffin used. (See Wax, page 39.)

An additional way of adding to or varying the amount of crackle in your design is to crumple the wax at various points in the dyeing process, either crumpling the entire batik or crumpling specific waxed areas of your design. In this way your whole batik will have a crackle texture, or certain areas of your design will have more crackle than other areas, thus giving variation and texture to your batik.

Technique · 117

Besides varying the amount of crackle in different parts of your design, you can also vary the *color* of the crackle from one part of your design to another. This is done by crumpling different parts of the cloth at different points in the dyeing process. For example, if you crumpled a waxed area of your batik before dyeing it blue, that area would have many blue cracks at this stage. If, after waxing the batik a second time, you crumpled an area that was white beneath the wax and then dyed the cloth red, the white area would have red cracks, and the area that, after the first dyeing, had many blue cracks would then have purple crackle. This is a technique of creating multicolored effects through the use of crackle.

Another way to vary color in your design through the use of crackle is to rewax areas between each dyebath in order to retain the color of the already existing crackle. For example, you have just dyed your fabric yellow, and in the process of your second waxing you rewax one particular white area. If you were now to dye the cloth red, the rewaxed area would retain its yellow crackle, whereas all the other crackle in the rest of the design would become orange. The basic point is that if you want to retain a certain color crackle, you must rewax the crackled area between each dye.

Using the *tjanting*, small and large brushes, and crackle to achieve the effects you desire takes time and practice. But learning the process itself is exciting and rewarding because as you develop your technique, the beauty of your batiks will also grow.

The Batik Process
from Start to Finish

To communicate to you the total experience of doing batik, we thought it would be helpful to describe the entire process from start to finish. In this way you will be able to see how each part fits into the whole, how all the aspects of the batik process that we have described before—fabric, wax, dye, design, color, and technique— take part in the activity itself. Also, our step-by-step description can be a guideline for you in doing your own batik so that you may avoid leaving out critical steps.

First you must decide what type of fabric you will work on—cotton, wool, or silk. If you choose cotton, you must wash it thoroughly, by hand or by machine, in order to remove sizing and other treatment it may have been exposed to. It may be necessary to wash it more than once. Washing must be done because any chemical treatment may interfere with the cloth absorbing the dye. Washing is not necessary with wool or silk, since they are not usually treated chemically in the same way as cotton. After washing it, hang the cloth to dry. When

119

it is dry, it is ready to be used (remember, the wax will not adhere to the cloth if it is wet). If the fabric is heavily wrinkled, you may want to press it, since this will facilitate stretching the fabric on the frame and waxing.

Next, if you are using a drawing for your design, transfer it from paper to the cloth itself, either by tracing or drawing freehand. Use a soft pencil. Meanwhile, heat your wax: fill the bottom of a double boiler with water, place it on a stove or hot plate, put wax (paraffin or beeswax) in the top of the double boiler, and turn the heat on. Or, as we prefer, place wax in an electric frying pan and turn the temperature control to about 300 or 325 degrees.

Prepare a worktable by covering it with paper (newspaper or newsprint is fine) to prevent the wax from dripping onto the table. Now stretch your fabric on a frame. You can buy a frame or make one yourself. The simplest and least expensive frame you can buy is artist's stretcher bars, designed for stretching a painter's canvas and available at any art-supply store. They come in various sizes and are easily put together and taken apart. By buying several pairs of stretcher bars in different lengths you can make different-sized frames. For example, if you buy pairs of 12-inch bars, 24-inch bars, and 30-inch bars, you can make frames of the following proportions: 12 x 24, 12 x 30, and 24 x 30. In addition to stretcher bars, you can purchase an adjustable frame for stretching cloth from Craftool, Inc. (See List of Suppliers, page 151.)

Another possibility is to build your own frame with wood and nails to the dimensions you desire. Generally, the size of the frame is determined by the width of the fabric. However, the frame can be smaller than the

OPPOSITE: *Frames for stretching batik come in several sizes.*

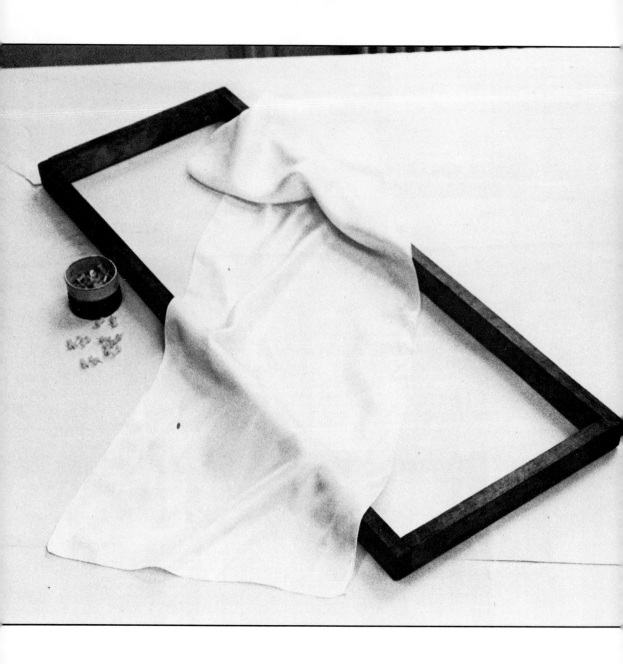

Try to use a frame about the size of your batik piece.

fabric used; in this case, the cloth must be moved from time to time as you are waxing.

When stretching the fabric on the frame, pull the cloth taut so that it will not touch and stick to the table as you apply the wax. Attach the cloth to the frame with thumbtacks or pushpins, but be careful that the pins or thumbtacks do not pull or tear the fabric, particularly a lightweight fabric. If you are working on fabric to be used for clothing, do not cut the pattern out first because it would then be more difficult, if not impossible, to stretch the fabric on the frame. The pattern pieces can be outlined on the cloth in pencil and then cut after the batik is completed.

Once the wax is melted, put your brushes and *tjanting* into your wax pot. The brushes will soften as they sit in the hot wax. When the wax is at the proper temperature (about 325 degrees) start applying the wax to your cloth. You can tell that the wax is the right temperature when it penetrates the cloth (look at both sides of the cloth); it is advisable to test the wax first on a scrap of fabric.

Remember that you are covering those areas with wax that you *do not* want to dye. If at this point—or at any other point in waxing your cloth—you accidentally drop wax where you had not planned, try to incorporate the "mistake" into your design. It is very difficult to remove the wax completely, but if you feel that the "mistake" really interferes with your design, you can try to remove it with benzene, with the iron-out technique, or by removing all the wax and starting your design again. (See Wax, page 39.)

When you have finished your first waxing, prepare your first dyebath. Follow the procedure for the particular dye you are using. It might be helpful to refer to the chapter on Dyes, page 53. The amount of dye you will use will depend on the intensity of color you want and, of course, on the quantity of fabric you are dyeing. Generally, the first dyebath should not be too intense,

The Batik Process from Start to Finish · 123

because you will dye over the first color several times. It is helpful to test the dyebath with a scrap of fabric to see if it is the color and intensity you want. If it is not, adjust the dyebath—add more water if it is too intense, or add more dye if it is too weak. You can add a little mild soap to your dyebath (Ivory or Lux liquid) to help the cloth absorb the dye. Finally, be sure to add all the chemical assistants (salt, acids, etc.) that are required for the particular dye you are using.

When your dyebath is ready, remove the cloth from the frame and prepare it for dyeing by wetting it in cold water. This will also help the cloth absorb the dye.

Put on rubber gloves and submerge the wet cloth in the dyebath. In order to ensure even dyeing, make an effort to submerge the entire piece of cloth at the same time and be sure to move the cloth around in the bath while it dyes. Leave the fabric in the dyebath for the length of time indicated in the instructions.

It is important to remember that when the cloth is wet, the color will look approximately twice as deep as it will look when it dries. This is especially true of cotton. So you should always dye the fabric to a shade twice as deep as you want it to be.

Dyeing is the time to consider crackle. If you want a lot of crackle in your design, crumple the cloth before placing it in the dye; if you want little or no crackle, try not to crumple the fabric and keep it as flat as possible while dyeing. Generally, do not crumple the fabric too much on the first dye—even if you desire a lot of crackle in the end—as each time you dye the cloth the resist will break and more crackle will be created.

Prepare a tub or bowl with clean, cold water in which to rinse the fabric. When you have finished dyeing the cloth, rinse it several times, each time in clean water, until little or no color comes out of the cloth. Now hang the cloth to dry, using plastic clothespins (wooden clothespins will absorb dye and sometimes spot your cloth). The cloth must be completely dry before you wax it again, or the wax will adhere to the fabric.

When it is dry, stretch your cloth on the frame again for a second waxing. This time you will wax in those areas that you wish to remain the color you have just dyed. For example, if the fabric was dyed yellow, you now wax those areas in your design you want to be yellow.

Once you have completed your second waxing, you will dye the cloth a second time, repeating the process of mixing dye, wetting the cloth, and dyeing the fabric as described above. Again hang the cloth to dry.

Stretch the fabric for a third waxing. Now you will wax only those areas you want to remain the color you have just dyed the fabric. Dye the cloth for a third time; follow the same procedure described in the first dyeing process. If this is to be the last dye, you might want to make a very strong bath to obtain an intense color. Once the cloth is dyed and rinsed, hang the cloth to dry.

If more colors are required in your design, continue the waxing and dyeing processes described above.

When you have dyed your cloth for the last time, and the cloth is thoroughly rinsed and dried, you are ready to remove the wax. At this point you will use one or a combination of the procedures for removing wax: ironing out, using a solvent, boiling, or dry-cleaning. (See Wax, page 39.)

THE BATIK PROCESS FROM START TO FINISH

Pictures are often the easiest way to explain any process. The following visual essay will explain the batik process a bit more clearly.

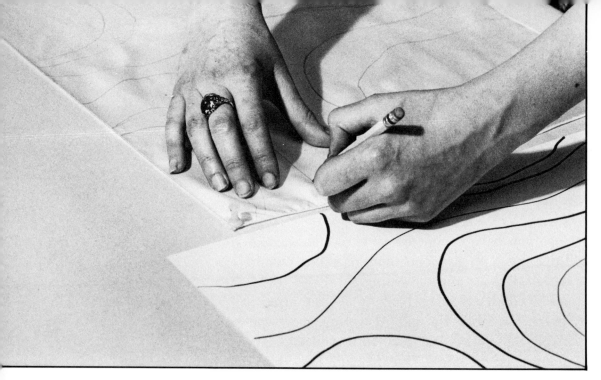

Transfer your design to fabric using a soft pencil.

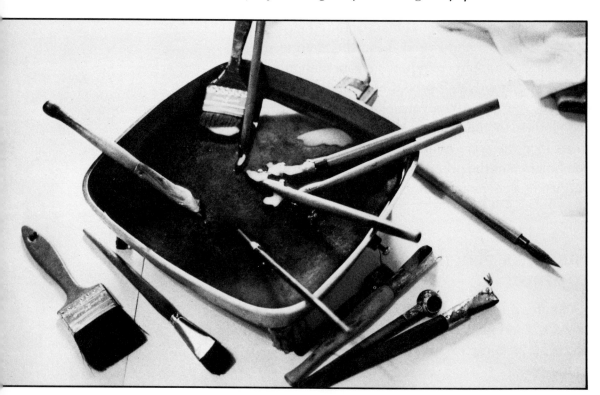

Melt paraffin or beeswax in a frying pan at 325°.

126

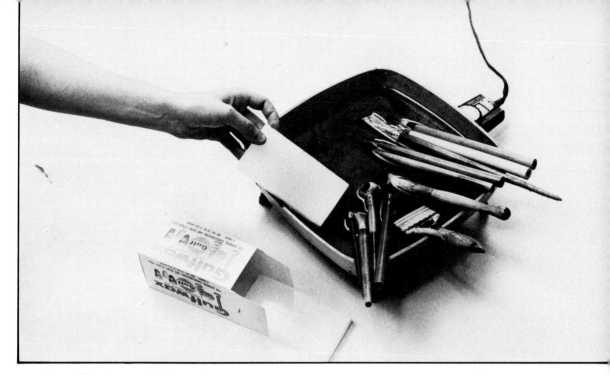

Brushes will soften in the heated wax.

Prepare your worktable by spreading paper or newsprint over it.

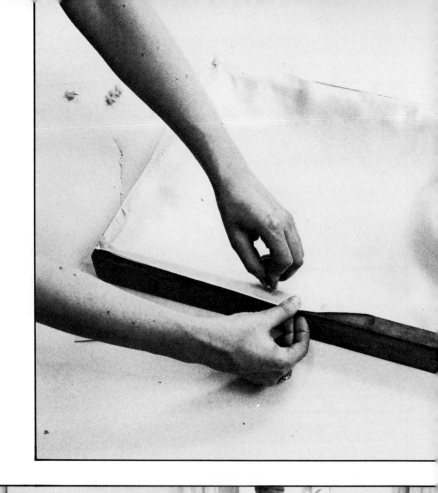

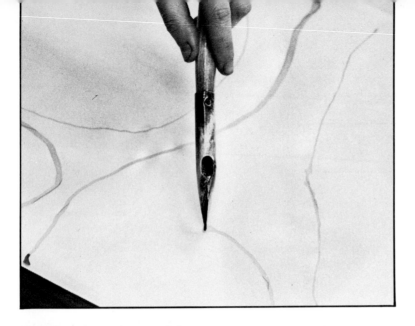

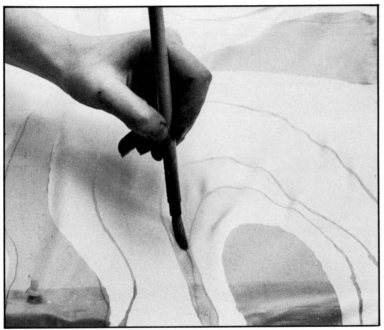

TOP LEFT: *Attach your fabric to the frame with pushpins.*

BOTTOM LEFT: *Be sure the fabric is taut on the frame.*

TOP: *Outline your design with a* tjanting.

BOTTOM: *Fill in the small areas with a thin brush, preferably an Oriental brush.*

129

Fill in large areas with a large brush.

Sometimes wax drips on your work, creating a "mistake."

Try to incorporate any "mistakes" into your design.

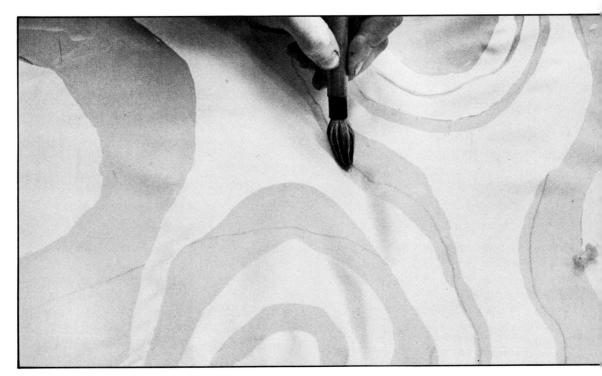

As a result, "mistakes" often add to a design rather than detract from it.

131

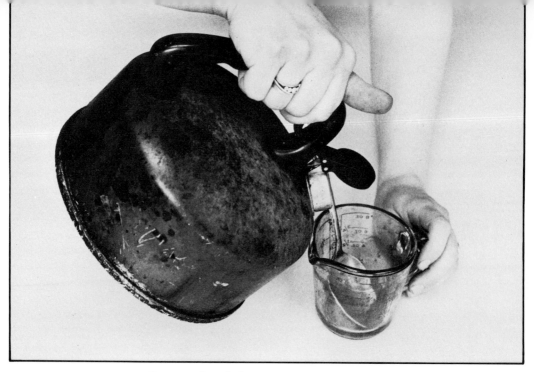

Put powdered dye in a measuring cup and dissolve it with boiling water.

Be sure the dye is completely dissolved.

Pour the dye solution into the basin you will use for dyeing.

Add water.

133

Opposite: *Add assistant, if necessary.*

Above: *Test to see that the dye is cool enough.*

Test the dye with a scrap of fabric.

The color should be twice as dark as you wish the finished piece.

OPPOSITE: Create extra crackle if you feel it is necessary.

LEFT: *Wet the batik piece in clear water before dyeing.*

RIGHT: *If you wish to avoid much crackle, keep your fabric as flat as possible.*

138

LEFT: *If you wish to create more crackle, squeeze the fabric in
the dyebath.*

RIGHT: *Transfer your dyed fabric to the rinsing basin.*

LEFT: *Rinse the fabric thoroughly.*

RIGHT: *Keep rinsing and rerinsing until no dye is left in the water.*

140

Hang to dry.

PART III
BATIK
IN MANY FORMS

Batik in Many Forms

When we first started writing this book, we were faced with certain considerations, one of which was "What should the title be?" And although certain problems were not easily solved (e.g., how does one write a sentence that is grammatically correct and at the same time communicates clearly aspects of the process of doing batik?), we knew our book would be entitled *Batik in Many Forms* before the writing began. After all, Batik in Many Forms was the name of our little batik center/business/studio for the three years preceding our writing venture, and our book was only to be a literary extension of what we had already been doing. But more importantly, we chose this title because it conveys a central idea and feeling we have about batik as a process, batik as a vehicle for an exploration of form.

Since so much of the experience of doing batik lies in exploring and experimenting with its different forms and functions, we thought we would end our book with a brief summary and review of the myriad forms batik can take. Many of these forms are shown photographically throughout the book; they might be useful to you as source ideas for your own work. But there is much more to batik than what you find in these pages. In doing your own work, you will discover this for yourself.

BATIK AS CLOTHING

Batik clothing has a special quality; it is original, personal, and one of a kind. Although perhaps not as practical as synthetic clothing, it is much more beautiful and meaningful because it is made by hand. Batik clothing brings beauty into your life rather than the dullness and boredom of ordinary throw-in-the-washing-machine cheap junk from the local bargain basement! Furthermore, if well cared for, batik clothing can last a lifetime. And the things you make with your batik will be things you will want to keep, that will never go out of style.

You can make skirts, blouses, dresses, scarves, coats, shawls, pants, purses. For men you can make shirts or ties, robes, handkerchiefs. You can make children's clothes, either for special party occasions, or for everyday run-around play. Batiked cotton T-shirts dyed with durable Procion dyes are both practical and unique. Children could even do their own batik for their own clothes!

BATIK FOR THE HOUSE

There is a multitude of uses for batik in home decorating, and the addition of batik will make any room more personal, colorful, and interesting. One of the special advantages of using batik in interior decorating is that you can pick up a particular motif or color scheme in the batik to enhance an overall feeling you wish to create. Or you can use batik as an accent or an additional textural effect. Whatever the case, some of the possible uses of batik in home decorating include pillows, wall hangings, curtains, room dividers, screens, lampshades, bedspreads, tablecloths, place mats, and upholstery.

BATIK AS GIFTS

The nicest gift is one that is made with your own hands and given with your heart. A batik in whatever form can serve as that kind of a gift. Obviously many of the forms of clothing or things for the home can also serve as gifts: scarves, pillows, tablecloths, or neckties, for example. In addition, batik dolls or stuffed animals are wonderful gifts which you can make and give to children or adults! Boxes covered with batik fabric, calendars, batik-covered diaries or sketch pads, bookmarks, cigarette or eyeglass cases—all are gifts that you can make by applying your skill and knowledge of the batik medium.

Whatever you use fabric for, you can use batik for. Hence batik offers endless possibilities and variations of form in relation to function. Not only does each new batik you work on allow you to experiment and explore design and color and technique, but each batik varies and presents new dimensions to your work by virtue of its function and application. In this way, batik as a medium is always exciting, challenging, experimental, explorative, and expansive. Batik is truly a craft—an art —of many forms.

APPENDICES

List of Suppliers

In general, frames, many of the less complex dyes, beeswax and wax mixtures, *tjantings,* and bamboo and standard brushes can be obtained from any local art-supply store. Most hardware and food stores carry paraffin. Despite the fact that natural-fiber fabrics are sometimes difficult to find, you should with a bit of looking be able to locate suitable fabric from a local fabric shop.

However, if you cannot find any of these essential materials for doing your batik, you can order them by mail from the following list of suppliers. You should always write for a price list or catalog before submitting an order.

Aiko's Art Materials
714 North Wabash
Chicago, Illinois 60611

Aiko's carries acid dyes, direct dyes, and *tjantings.*

Aljo Manufacturing
    Company, Inc.
116 Prince Street
New York,
    New York 10012

Aljo's carries their own brand-name dyes, which include both acid dyes and direct dyes. They also sell beeswax, wax mixtures, and *tjantings*.

Jerry Brown Imported
   Fabrics, Inc.
37 West 57th Street
New York,
   New York 10019

Jerry Brown's is a source for natural fabrics, especially cotton and silk.

Craftool, Inc.
1421 West 240th Street
Harbor City,
   California 90710

Craftool sells their own brand-name dyes, which include both acid dyes and direct dyes. They also sell paraffin, beeswax, bamboo and standard brushes, *tjantings*, frames, and even natural fabrics.

W. Cushing & Company
Dover-Foxcroft,
   Maine 04426

Cushing's sells their own brand-name dyes (Cushing's Perfection), which

are all-purpose dyes. They also sell wax and *tjantings*.

Far Eastern Fabrics, Inc.
171 Madison Avenue
New York,
   New York 10016

Natural silk and cotton can be ordered.

Horikoshi, Incorporated
109 West 38th Street
New York,
   New York 10016

Natural silk and cotton can be ordered.

Sam Flax
25 East 28th Street
New York,
   New York 10016

   Or any of their branch stores:

Sam Flax
551 Madison Avenue
New York,
   New York 10022

Sam Flax
3021 Peachtree Road
Atlanta, Georgia 30305

Sam Flax
51 West Grand Avenue
Chicago, Illinois 60610

Sam Flax
250 Sutter Street
San Francisco,
   California 94108

Sam Flax
10852 Lindbrook Drive
Los Angeles,
   California 96024

Sam Flax sells virtually all batik supplies except fabric: Sennelier dyes, Fibrec dyes, frames, bamboo and standard brushes, *tjantings*, paraffin, and beeswax.

Pylam Products
95-10 218th Street
Queens Village,
   New York 11429

Pylam sells procion and other fiber-reactive dyes.

Screen Process Supplies
1199 East 12th Street
Oakland, California 94606

Inko dyes, *tjantings*, and Indian Head cotton can be ordered.

Suggested Reading

Books

Deyrup, Astrith. *Getting Started in Batik*. New York: Macmillan Publishing Co., Inc., 1971.

Gibbs, Joanifer. *Batik Unlimited*. New York: Watson-Guptill Publications, 1974.

Keller, Ila. *Batik: The Art & Craft*. Rutland, Vermont: Charles E. Tuttle, Inc., 1966.

Krevitsky, Nik. *Batik: Art & Craft*. New York: Van Nostrand Reinhold Company, 1973.

Martin, Beryl. *Batik for Beginners*. New York: Charles Scribner's Sons, 1972.

Meilach, Dona Z. *Contemporary Batik & Tie-Dye*. New York: Crown Publishers, Inc., 1972.

Nea, Sara. *Batik: Materials, Techniques, Design*. New York: Van Nostrand Reinhold Company, 1972.

Samuel, Evelyn. *Introducing Batik*. New York: Watson-Guptill Publications, 1968.

Shaw, Jennifer & Shaw, Robin. *Batik: New Look at an Ancient Craft*. Doubleday Publishing Company, 1974.

Pamphlets

Coloristic Aspects of African Prints, by Ing W. Kretz-
schmar. Reprint from Meillian Textiberichte, Vol.
10, 1970.

The Writing of Batik. Published by Craftools, Inc., 1421
240th Street, Harbor City, California 90710.

Inko Dye. Published by Screen Process Supplies, 1199
East 12th Street, Oakland, California.

Index